Understanding
Children Writing

D1290650

Carol Burgess, Tony Burgess, Liz Cartland, Robin Chambers,
John Hedgeland, Nick Levine, John Mole, Bernard Newsome,
Harold Smith, Mike Torbe

Penguin Education

Penguin Education
A Division of Penguin Books Ltd
Harmondsworth, Middlesex, England
Penguin Books Inc, 7110 Ambassador Road,
Baltimore, Md 21207, USA
Penguin Books Australia Ltd,
Ringwood, Victoria, Australia

First published 1973
Copyright © Carol Burgess, Tony Burgess, Liz Cartland, Robin Chambers,
John Hedgeland, Nick Levine, John Mole, Bernard Newsome,
Harold Smith, Mike Torbe, 1973

Made and printed in Great Britain by
Richard Clay (The Chaucer Press) Ltd,
Bungay, Suffolk
Set in Monotype Times

Penguin Education
Understanding Children Writing

Carol Burgess, Tony Burgess, Liz Cartland, Robin Chambers,
John Hedgeland, Nick Levine, John Mole, Bernard Newsome,
Harold Smith, Mike Torbe

Contents

Preface

This book has grown out of work which some of us did in preparation for the Annual Conference of the National Association for the Teaching of English on 'Language Across the Curriculum' in 1971. A kind of trial run for the book appeared in the 1971 conference issue of *English in Education* as the section headed 'Kinds of Writing'. We have expanded considerably from that early beginning. More people have joined us; more material has been collected; more pupils in more schools have been asked to help. We have also expanded the framework and attempted to make a collection of wider interest, intended to help towards an understanding of the way writing abilities develop and of the range of different kinds of writing.

We have worked on the book as a group, and all of it (except the last section) reflects something of all of us. We have agreed, however, to bury in this preface some of the lines of individual responsibility. The major part of the work has been divided up as follows:

Introduction and some final tidying: Tony Burgess

Part One: Bernard Newsome

Part Two: Carol Burgess, Liz Cartland, Robin Chambers, John Mole

Part Three: John Hedgeland, Nick Levine, Harold Smith, Mike Torbe

Part Four: John Hedgeland (Michael), Bernard Newsome (Kerry), Robin Chambers (Chris), Carol and Tony Burgess (Jessica)

Part Five: Harold Smith, Mike Torbe

Part Six reflects actual practice in the classroom, and for this reason we have retained the names of the compilers.

Acknowledgements are due to the Schools Council Writing Research Unit for permission to reproduce the following pieces of writing: in Section 1, number 3; in Section 3, number 16; in Section 4, all Kerry's writing; in Section 5, numbers 6 to 20 inclusive.

We have tried to trace the authors of all the writing reproduced, but in some cases this has not proved possible. We would be very pleased to hear from people we have missed. In reproducing the writing we have in all cases preserved the original spelling, punctuation, paragraphing and so on. Diagrams, on the other hand, have been redrawn except where otherwise stated.

Finally our thanks are due to Mrs Sara Mark who read the book in manuscript and to Miss Nancy Martin and Professor James Britton who similarly read the manuscript and encouraged us during its preparation. Our debt to Miss Martin and Professor Britton and more generally to the work of the Writing Research Unit of the University of London Institute of Education is simply stated. There is little we have learned which we have not learned from them. What we have done with it is another matter.

Introduction

This is a book, not of Children's Writing, but of children writing. Let me clarify that emphasis. We are used to the fact that children can write with astonishing quality. Anyone who finds this questionable had better turn straight to some of the writing in the section in this book called 'Sharing Experience' (or to Alec Clegg's *The Excitement of Writing*, 1964, or Robert Druce's *Eye of Innocence*, 1965, to name but two alternatives): he will find there plenty to make the point to him. But then the run of school writing was never quite caught by that kind of undertaking. Indeed that was the point of the books. They were powerful beacons – lights that could guide us if we set our course by them, or at least reminders that there was light if we could only lift our noses a bit and look at it. But it was never their intention to give an idea of the general range of the writing children had to do in school or which was expected of them.

Ours is a more workaday interest. We haven't set out to convince anyone that children can write splendidly (partly we take it as given) nor are we arguing any specific sort of approach, though we *are* convinced of certain general thoughts about writing. Mainly we were interested just to see what it is actually like to be someone learning to write, to see what sort of things he is asked to do and to represent to ourselves something of what is involved in learning to do them. Children after all are called on to write an incredible amount during the course of their school career. My guess, based on a look at one secondary school, is that an average fourth-former covers between fifty and sixty sides of quarto paper a week with some sort of writing or other. The figure may cause some surprise. Actually nobody knows enough to say how average this is. Whatever truth may be in it, the thought remains that learning to write must be for most children a central and in some ways the most ambiguous fact of their school experience. We were interested in pinning it down.

But we wanted predominantly to show the writing itself, rather than our thoughts about it. For we felt pretty much that if we let that writing speak for itself we would be doing most service to the people who shared our interest. They could then make up their own minds and see for themselves. There is an invitation in this of course which stands throughout the book. It is meant more to be thought about than imbibed.

This anthology then, is meant to be broadly representative of the run of writing in school. Having said that I had better qualify any impression that it is wholly comprehensive. We have tried not to leave anything out which people might have wanted to see in, but of course there are things which go on in schools which are not represented here. We could not bring ourselves, for example, to include any of the mass of answers to questions, exercises and so on which still form a substantial part of many children's diet. Also the people who have worked on this book have all of them been teachers and all but three are still actively teaching. Thus, much of the writing has been contributed by children whom they have taught. No doubt it reflects some of their teachers' preoccupations, their emphases and some of their successes. (We have not set out to document the failures of the school system of which we are as conscious as anybody.) Not all the writing has been gathered from our own sources: some, good and bad, has come from other places. But a large part has come from us, and the book as a whole reflects a little bit the sort of teachers we have been – it could hardly have been otherwise.

My purpose now, though, is to say something about the interests and assumptions which have guided us in gathering the collection, at the same time to raise some issues which people may care to take with them into the book. With a nice piquancy I must settle to write about writing.

We need an image of the writer.

Pretty well of necessity he sits alone. Book or paper in front of him, an implement to work with. But the rest of the world's apparatus – all its entries and exits, confrontations and demands – sinks into remoteness. The stage on which he acts is one on which no one watches him acting. Only indirectly is he aware of other people – as potential auditors of the slow accumulation of the voice he hears inside him. For the present, life proceeds line by line. We, on the other hand, as we watch him, detect a rhythm to his behaviour. There are long periods when he sits, motionless, staring in front of him, nothing apparently going on. Instead he may stand, walk about, light pipe or cigarette, chew (or sniff rotten apples, if all the stories are to be believed). But then there is another rhythm – a dipping of the head, a tension in the body (sometimes it is an almost ludicrous contortion), and a mere line of black marks which he has won from silence.

It is a strange mixture of the romantic and the ridiculous. There is the remoteness of the writer and the twofold rhythm of his labour – those long immobile stares while the inward eye searches for thoughts and meanings, then the jerk towards the physical act as the meanings are transferred to paper. That it may seem romantic derives no doubt from the sense of a virtually infinite possibility in the written word (it is an old theme); ridiculous because of the oddity of the means at the writer's disposal. What is going on, though, more precisely? For the outward signs, of course, the physical means, will not get us very far. We need to penetrate the act, to speculate our way towards – and it is essentially speculative – the terms in which the act takes place in the writer's consciousness.

Let me try and speculate introspectively. As I write this now I am caught in the gap between where I have been and where I must go and there is no one at hand to help me. I have the inner circle of my readers – others within the group of us (co-planners now turned readers) – they will be watching me perform. But they are not to hand. Also, though I have to satisfy them, it is not with them that I have to engage. That engagement is reserved for you. To you whom I do not know I have to reach out as though I did. I partly know what I have to say but only partly: it is latent in me, not yet endowed with style within my head. It is open to me only to press forward hopefully, modifying myself the better that you may engage with me.

But if this is all rather special it is so in degree rather than kind. There is nothing here that, given allowances for a different situation, any writer would not have to cope with. Any writer will have to find a way of thinking about a reader whom he can see in his mind but not in his eye. He will have to move from a meaning which he reaches for to one he may fully grasp only when he has written it. Any writer will have to cope with the fact that what he has written has gone out from him into the world. He hopes that it may be valued; he knows that it will be assessed. He hopes too that he will like it himself when he comes to see it again.

Writing then is not easy. Putting it more systematically it imposes demands on the performer which do not characterize in the same way either our other *active* use of language (talking) or our *receptive* ones (reading and listening). Talk, characteristically speaking, flows from us. Potentially it may be attended by many of the same difficulties, but in practice we often barely notice them. There are times when writing is relatively easy. (I can pay my electricity bill without linguistic agony and usually manage a page or so to a friend before I falter.) But there are always at the heart of writing things which I can take for granted some of the time but which are never far from rising into my consciousness as problems.

At its simplest I have to transfer words which exist for me as strings of soundless formulations in the head into an accumulating set of marks on paper. Old at the game now, I can do this relatively easily. But for children (I am reminding myself rather than you) this transfer from a medium which is primarily aural to a medium which is primarily visual is something which has initially to be learned explicitly, and is thereafter for a long time complicated. Even as an adult I make mistakes. For my own part I tend to omit words rather than mis-spell, for if I give my attention exclusively to the visual record which I leave behind me, it interferes with all the other things I have to do.

At the same time I have to analyse my utterance into sentences as I form it and permit to myself only such length or form of utterance as I can neatly marshal. This is not a matter of explicit grammatical knowledge, of knowing what a sentence is. For grammar is not quite like that and nor is writing. Rather, it is the feel for what I want to say, for the unit of my meaning. In talk I can launch myself in hope, and hope to come out the other end. I can begin, stop in the middle, wonder if . . . well, no . . . and so, participles trailing, arrive at my listener's mercy. Readers are intolerant of such diversions. Much, too, that I can leave implicit and unsaid in talk I have to formulate in writing. Add to this that we expect of the written word, in most forms, a much tighter grammatical structuring. It is not surprising that what children can write is often much simpler than what they can speak; nor that in the endeavour to transfer to writing the complexity of the ideas they can handle in talk or 'in the head', they sometimes launch themselves without arriving. It is so for all of us.

Linguists call such failures to arrive 'mazes'. The presence of such 'mazes' (of which we are much more tolerant in talk), points to a general difficulty characteristic of all utterance but particularly marked in writing: we cannot wholly know or evaluate what we are going to say until we have said it. In the process of utterance we have to cope with many different levels of problem all at once. The writer in fact is like a man before one of those (Science Fiction) space control units at the moment when the Martians arrive. At all conceivable points on the machine the lights flash and the noises buzz, while our hero wrestles with the one bit of it he can give his attention to. The fundamental problem with children writing is not so much that children find it difficult, but that it is difficult for everyone.

It was our sense of this complexity which led us to include, as a major concern of the book, our later section on 'The Difficulties of Writing'. In that section we try to document some of those cases where writing goes wrong. I hope, though, that it also tends to document one of our fundamental feelings: that we need to locate the difficulties which children find in learning to write in the nature of writing as well as in the children.

Sometimes we have been apt to talk a bit globally about the less able child (or whatever) without always fully evaluating what he was less able at.

Let me turn in more detail to the processes involved in writing. We might, for example, think of it as something relatively mechanical. There are times when writing is very close to being merely this. But then even the most mechanical activity has to be sustained by an act of personal commitment on the part of the actor. I would like to try and get the nature of that commitment clearer. It is not to some general 'value of writing' that the writer is committed. That for him is a matter to be settled before or after, when there is time to switch to another way of thinking, to stand back and take stock. What matters *at the time* is that there is enough investment in it to make it worthwhile carrying on. And the investment, strictly speaking, is not in something external – in the rewards which will follow, or the pleasure some reader will take – but in what is coming up as the writing is going on, in the thoughts which are arriving in the head. Like climbing a hill – it is nice to stand at the bottom and think about the top and nice to stand at the top and think about what one has done. But the doing has to be sustained as it goes along, by the hundreds of minute acts at each of which the labourer can withdraw his labour. Or, think of the time which boys give to football. It is not the consequences which make it worthwhile, but the involvement in it. Nor is it the chance to learn to be a better footballer. And though we have to learn to write, it is not what we can learn about writing which, at any one moment, settles our involvement in it.

There is another point too about the nature of this commitment which is more difficult to express. I can come at it if I try to specify more precisely the link between the drive of the writer's central concern (a process which goes on inside the head) and the outcome of that drive – that is to say, the written marks on paper which are the record of it. We talk sometimes for example of 'searching for words'. The metaphor is helpful in so far as it reminds us that words do not come instantaneously. But it is unhelpful if it betrays us into thinking that it is words we actually search for, rather than the meanings which words have it in them to formulate. Embarrassed before a friend or dilapidated on my return home at night, words may fail me where the person who confronts me has no such problem. But I would find the words if I could find the meaning which would do the trick. Thus, being at a loss for words, strictly speaking, is not so much a matter of not having the words ready at hand for the job, as of not being able in the stress of the situation to represent to oneself the sort of job that the words ought to be doing. The writer too, while he calls up words into his head and while, to a greater or lesser extent, he feels his way about in them, assessing their power before committing them to paper, can be described as being attentive to words only in so far as they are the medium for his real commitment, his commitment to the meaning he searches to articulate.

The bearing of this point, which at first sight may seem a bit finicky, has its practical importance. Many of us, I suppose, may have sensed a possible conflict in all this. On the one hand we might recognize the importance of this active involvement on the part of the writer; on the other we might wonder how this was compatible in practice with children achieving quality in their writing. For there is an old adage that 'practice make perfect' and practice is something which is pursued characteristically separate from the activity which is practised for. But if we read the relation between words and meanings aright I do not think we could ever set out to develop qualities in children's writing as a matter of practice, to improve, for example, their powers of description by a course in descriptive writing. Nor could we just pass on to children words and concepts without a prior commitment on their part to the meanings those words are there to formulate. Not that there might not be marginal gains from the attempt. We would have a hard time, though, knowing how direct the gains were. Such gains too would be insignificant in comparison with what a child learns from his general exposure to language as he goes about his business. But every time we did this we would be getting in the way of a real sense of the nature of the writing activity developing. For the priority would remain getting real writing going in real situations where a real commitment to the search for meaning becomes possible.

For words are things we see through rather than things in which we rest: that is to say they are symbols rather than objects, an element on which we float – or, more appropriately, swim – rather than one in which we are immersed. They ask not to be practised but to be used. Or think again of boys playing football and the relation of all that activity, all that running and passing and kicking, and the background of rules in the head of each player – the relation of all that to the centrally held objective of scoring. So in writing, as James Britton (1970) has put it, it is on the objective that the writer keeps his eye, while at the same time trying to get, and keep, the flow of language going.

And there is of course an irreducible difficulty at the heart of writing – the point where all the other difficulties, with the system, the syntax, the lexis, the conventions – where all these meet. Quite simply it is that the search for meaning *is* a search, that it cannot be known until it is found, that it is not till the labour is completed that one can know whether it was worth it. And sometimes it isn't. Perhaps if there is any one thing that we can do to help children in learning to write it is to prevent them from having to face that reality too harshly. For the confidence to make a journey depends on a reasonable assumption that the end will be reached and that it will be worth it. It seems a pity that sometimes in school it is not this move which is made but another: that of so priming children in the information which must be included, even in the way it must be organized, that the personal search for meaning is once again turned into an exercise.

To focus this sense of the writer's commitment more exactly I shall need to relate it to another component in the writing process. Let me invent a word for this and speak of the way in which a writer comes to *frame* his task. When I say invent a word (it is hardly a very new invention) I mean simply that I need a word which will pick out as a single activity on the part of the writer what is in fact the product of very many diverse factors at work. I mean too that it is helpful to think of it as a single activity and that we may well not have a generally accepted word for it, because while it is something a writer does he may often not make his doing of it very explicit to himself.

I need, though, to take account of the fact that writings vary. They vary in difficulty; in the extent to which they draw on the resources of the spoken or written language; in the degree to which the writer can develop or subordinate himself in the act of writing; in the degree to which he must be formal or colloquial – and no doubt in many other ways as well. Such widely differing uses of language are an important fact about the general context of culture on which the writer has to draw. We need to take account of the fact too that any piece of writing is conceived within a specific situation, making particular demands on the writer which he has to meet.

For the freedom of the writer is not absolute, nor is he as bare-headed before each new writing task as my previous account might have seemed to imply. Cut off though he may be, he still writes within a situation: his writing has an immediate context. New though each new task may be to him as a problem, he has his previous experience of language in all its varieties – writing, talking, listening and reading – on which to draw. Thus there are factors both outside him and within him which can help him to a start. From them he can construct a framework within which the task can be fulfilled, which, like the frameworks of physical construction, limit the space which is to be occupied, but at the same time enable the possibilities which can go on within it. Out of the link which the writer makes between a situation, which is given from without, and his resources and experience of language within, he *frames* his task, sets up for himself the limits and possibilities within which his search for meaning can take place.

Think first of the situation in which the writer finds himself. Clearly there are many different forms which it may take. Clearly also it may be so ordered that the writer is content to be directed by it, to accept for the moment the terms it offers. Or he may wish to resist it, to offer his writing in defiance of it. Alternatively, he might fall a victim merely to his failure to understand or meet its expectations. Situations, like writings, vary. But we can get some order into that flux of possible difference by focusing three elements within the writer's situation. Firstly, there is the topic with which the writer has to deal. It may be about himself, about things which have happened to him or the person he is; or, too, about things which possibly might happen or the person he might possibly be. Autobiography or fiction must start from somewhere here. Alternatively, it may be about objective fact, about things which exist in the world outside him, beyond the accident of his personal experience or the possibility of his imaginative contrivance. And here again the topic may call for what he fairly confidently knows or for something on the borders of what he knows with confidence, about which he must be more exploratory. We explore further this very broad division – between the self and the objective world – in Parts Two and Three ('Sharing Experience' and 'Handling Information').

Thus the topic represents one element in the writer's situation. Secondly, there is the person (or persons) for whom he is to write and his knowledge of their expectations. There are many possibilities here. Is it a single person he is addressing or several? Does he feel himself close to his audience or distant? Must he be intimate or detached? What sort of person must he show himself to be in writing for them? Can he be himself, as it were (which bit of himself?) or must he take up some sort of role – of deference or aggression, of entertainer or of solemnity, of historian, even, or scientist? Whatever are the roles and possibilities here will affect the way in which he frames his task, sometimes even his capacity to do so.

Thirdly, there are the physical means and possibilities at his disposal and their limits. This is no trivial matter. Any writer will have to come to terms with the length in which his meaning must be encompassed and with what sort of time is available. Can he be the determiner of this or are there limits which he must meet from outside? For this will affect the way he writes. What is at his disposal to use? Can he use pictures and diagrams? Can he be the determiner of the form his output is to take, such that he can make a book, or conceive it for display on the wall, or to be read aloud to a group or by one person at a time silently? There is a range of possibilities here whose directions and importance I can do no more than indicate.

Let me pause now to draw a few of my threads together. I began with a sense of the problems the writer has to face. He has to deal with the writing system and exploit the resources of the grammar much more systematically than he has to in talk. He has, too, in any act of writing to locate himself in terms of his relations with his readers and their expectations as to the kind of thing he is writing. Ability of the second kind involves the penetration of an entire social order. Thus we can contrast two kinds of learning involved in learning to write: the relatively specific learning involved in mastering the elements of spelling and so on, and the much more general learning involved in the ability to write effectively in various kinds of discourse. The latter can only be the outcome of the extensive accumulation of resources over a long period of time. On the other hand there is also the point that the writer needs not only to have the resources but also to be able to mobilize them. What then are the components of the writing process which underlie the writer's mobilization of his resources? I have focused two of them: first, the commitment to a search for meaning; second, a framing of that commitment in terms of the situation which the writer has to meet.

I need, though, in order to complete my account, some sort of total sense of the resources of the written language. For I have described the writer's framing of his task as the link he makes between the situation he confronts and the resources he has at his disposal. Equally, if we are to find some way of charting the development of children in their writing we need to be able to represent the totality of uses to which the written language can be put. In the past, perhaps, we have had only a rather rough and ready method of conceptualizing these. Teachers have had to rely either on rather global contrasts, distinguishing, for example, between personal and impersonal uses of language, informal or formal, private or public; or else they have had to locate simply the sort of writing appropriate to a particular academic subject and set out to develop that. Relying on the one offered some sort of general theory at the expense of much in the way of insight. Relying on the other neglected any general sense of the total possibilities of the written language in favour of concentrating on a number of particular uses.

Recently the Writing Research Unit (Institute of Education, London)* has developed a more detailed account. It underlies to a large extent the way we have planned this book, and while this is not the place to expound it fully, let me give a brief account of its basic thinking.

Broadly that account distinguishes between different types of writing in terms of the *functions* which language may serve. For function we may understand 'purposes'. It then develops a model of these functions in which the three principal categories are as follows:

* Acknowledgements are due to my colleagues past and present at the Writing Research Unit: Professor James Britton, Miss Nancy Martin, Dr Harold Rosen, Messrs Denis Griffiths, Alex McLeod, Peter Medway, Bernard Newsome and Harold Smith.

1. Transactional
2. Expressive
3. Poetic

The diagram locates the relations between them:

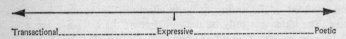

Transactional_____Expressive_____Poetic

The conception of the expressive function of language occupies a central place in the account. Traditionally, the idea of 'expressive' language has carried with it connotations of the expression of emotion, even of self-expression. In this account it is given a more flexible definition in terms of the language of intimate exchange. Expressive talk between friends is characteristically informal and relaxed, much of its meaning is left implicit by the speaker who assumes on the part of the listener a willingness to enter into his purposes. Expressive writing carries over these assumptions from speech. Here is an example:

15th feb. Monday. first we had Register and then Mrs. L and Mrs. S had a big mone and then we had movement, well all the rest of the class did I had something rong with my ears. after that we went out to play and then we got to work I had to do my story. then we had dinner then we went out to play and then we had halltime then we had to do our work which was mathematics and story and then we all talked about things and then we all went home.

Expressive writing is a function of language which is capable of development in its own right, but it occupies a central place diagrammatically since it is seen also as the matrix of other functions of language. Thus the language of the young child may not move much outside the expressive function. As he develops he not only enriches his use of that function, but becomes able to move on from the expressive in either a transactional or a poetic direction.

Beneath the term *transactional* are incorporated all the *informative* and *persuasive* uses of language (the account gives a number of sub-divisions of these). This is the language of the philosopher and the scientist. The term transactional is used to pick out the fact that as a writer modifies his expressive language in this direction he does so in order to take up a transaction in the objective world outside him, to deal with facts and theory and information. Thus:

Woodside Farm is the same as any other farm on the south-western slopes of New South Wales. The Owner is Mr. Murphy which was started by his father in 1913.

The farm covers 1,400 acres which is used for cattle and crops. 900 acres are used for oats and wheat and the rest for the 2,450 Merino sheep which are owned by Mr. Murphy

For different purposes, though, the writer may modify his expressive language in a *poetic* direction. In this direction lie the uses of language as an art-form, where the formal qualities of language become of central importance and where the writer's concern becomes with the creation of a verbal object such as a poem, a novel or a play. This too represents a modification of the writer's expressive language, but for a different purpose, and hence it is modified in different ways:

rotifers
and bitten coasts
threshed seaweeds
and drenched noise
slow moving barnacles
and quick insistent surf
speak in a timeless language
of a period of time
they have seen
though not I
of
rotifers
and bitten coasts
threshed seaweeds
and drenched noise
slow moving barnacles
and quick insistent surf

For a fuller account of this the reader must be referred elsewhere (Britton, 1971). It is enough for my purposes now if I note that there are many kinds of writing, but not so many that we cannot get some sort of picture of them; also that the account offers a way of seeing the total resources of the writer (potentially) at the point where he confronts his task In Part Four ('Four Pupils and Their Writing') we attempt to trace something of the pattern by which the writer develops these powers. But there is much still that we simply do not know.

Let me close by attempting to face squarely the issue of how children learn to write. Before the child learns to write he learns to talk – and we know a certain amount about the way that ability is acquired. We know for example that he acquires his syntax by a process of refinement; that in the beginning his 'telegraphic' utterances, two words in length, contain only two very general grammatical classes; that as he develops these classes are refined and developed into others (Brown and Bellugi, 1964). We know too that talk about the way in which the child acquires language which sees the central process in terms of imitation, or alternatively in coming to associate words with certain things, misdirects us as to the kind of thing language is. Rather we have to give a central place to the fact that the child has to interpret the language that he hears about him, that he has to feel his way, essentially experimentally, towards its rules, and that he learns it in the context of his own world, his own purposes and his own meanings.

There is little reason to suppose that the process of learning to write is radically different. He has of course to master the writing *system* – a relatively specific matter. Thereafter his development as a writer depends on his general acquiring of resources and his ability to mobilize them in specific writing tasks. As the work of the Writing Research Unit suggests, his writing is likely to develop from that which relies most closely on the resources of speech (and story) to encompass an increasing range of different kinds.

It is to the active use of language, therefore, that I would give central emphasis. I had better make clear the sense in which I mean this. There is of course a sense in which all writing is active: it is something we do, not something we experience. If that was all I meant I would mean very little. I mean by active the sense that the writer controls the possibilities of his own language, that he can use his writing to act on his situation, appropriating it in terms of his own meaning rather than accepting that of another. I would oppose an active use of writing firstly to being controlled by somebody else, secondly to merely routine performances.

This is a rather more formidable thought – though one, I believe we need to face. For in the past in schools the role of the teacher has sometimes dominated that of the learner. Children have been expected to become committed to an activity in which the adult controlled the topic which they could write about and the way in which they could write about it, was himself the audience for whom they could write, himself limited the physical means at the writer's disposal to a few pages in an exercise book, limited the time which was available to a set period and determined the point at which writing became relevant in a given period of learning. It was left only for the child to perform. It was hardly surprising that the world became divided into those who could cope with these conditions and those who could not – or did not care to.

Schools are moving out of this situation. On the other hand, if we are to do more than simply leave children alone, we need to accompany this move with a developing sense of the range of possibilities. I believe that to look for ways in which children can write for people outside the teacher might be a profitable direction. They could write, for example, for their contemporaries, either within their own particular teaching group, or for another group or for a group in another school. Or they could write for a relatively public audience outside the school, for parents or friends. And if the teacher became one in a range of possible audiences this would enable him to play a more positive and defined role. For if writing in this way for more public audiences gives a measure of reality to the activity, it is arguable that children need too the more personalized help which only a single adult can give. For I realize that they need to try things out too, to experiment and test themselves in a situation which is not critical. In an extended range of possibilities we as adults could set ourselves more firmly towards developing confidence rather than assessing a performance.

How, in fact, can we leave room for children to follow their own meanings and to frame their writing in their own way in situations which are not dominated by the authority of the teacher alone? It is a pressing question, particularly for writing which seeks to inform. Probably the major proportion of the writing which children at present do is of this kind. The major weight of the curriculum viewed as a whole is towards developing it. But in the past much of the informative writing which went on in schools hardly sought genuinely to inform so much as to indicate to the relevant authority that the relevant information has been mastered. In this situation writing of a very limited kind tended to develop. Its duty was firstly to the facts of the case rather than to the theories or range of theories which those facts might invite. It had to be rigorously objective, in the sense not merely that the writing had to deal with matters of objective truth, but that all attempts to develop a personal context for those truths, which made some attempt to come to terms with their interest and value had to be suppressed. It was usually possible to write only once and in one kind of way on any given topic.

It was not simply that the sort of writing we have called transactional became the main kind of writing in schools, but it was very much transactional of a certain type – reports, for example, or classifications of facts, in which no personal or speculative voice ever appeared.

If we are to go beyond this, then, we need a sense here of the range of possibilities. The categories of the Writing Research Unit which I have mentioned offer us a start. I should have expected young writers to have made much more use of that sort of writing which they call expressive (tentative personal writing which carries forward the resources of speech) than at present appears to be the case. I suspect that it is often inhibited. It is a part of learning to come to distinguish between the objective facts of the case and the accidental features of the situation in which those facts were first met. Even for the mature writer, though, it may be that expressive writing affords a chance to make explicit in a first draft those processes of thinking which the demand for an immediate objective presentation would force him to leap. The immature writer may have no option.

Is it, anyway, with an objective presentation of the facts that the writing should stop? There is this end to be looked at too. Not only older writers (though they particularly) would want to use their writing to examine the theories which facts make possible, to follow the speculations which open up from learning, even to incorporate fact and theory within the personal contexts of their beliefs. Yet one has to search in school to find writing which is of this sort. I suspect that this is too inhibited. Why, too, does there seem to be so little concern for poem and story outside the English class-room? I should have thought that it is not in English alone that imaginative entry into experience is required.

Further thoughts along these lines are developed by Harold Rosen in 'Towards a language policy across the curriculum' (Barnes, Britton, Rosen and the LATE, 1971). But it is time now to give way to the other voices of the book. Let me say a word more about it. We started by attempting to give some sense of the range of possible Kinds of Writing before passing to illustrate in more detail two general directions which writing may take ('Sharing Experience' and 'Handling Information'). Then we try to illustrate something of the way children develop as writers ('Four Pupils and Their Writing'). We look then at what is difficult about writing ('Difficulties of Writing'). Finally we offer a range of accounts which attempt to chart something of the relationship between writing and talk in specific 'Contexts'.

There are many reasons why we should value children learning to write. Lest we be thought not to see the wood for the trees let me say that we recognize that it is not the only symbolic means at our disposal, that we can draw, paint, write music, play, model and mime as well – all of them ways in which we can re-enter our experience symbolically and give it meaning. We recognize too that many of these ways are more accessible than writing. Talk in particular invites spontaneity, is less rigorous in its syntactical demands. Sentences can be left trailing, thoughts begun and left unfinished, meaning left implicit – for the listener is there and present to enter intuitively into the speaker's purposes. It permits too intonation and gesture which have to be jettisoned in writing. More important than any of this it eases the burden on the writer of the necessity for sustained

utterance and of his isolation from the reassuring nod or friendly intervention. The writer has to leave all this behind him.

But then the isolation of the writer also has its rewards. Removed from
the cut and thrust of conversation he can ponder much more slowly what
he has to say. Also he can sustain his thinking over a much longer period –
or almost indefinitely, as in *War and Peace*, for example – for he can return
continually to what he has written before and pick up the threads. There is
no-one to interrupt him or to pose some other topic. Thus the writer is free
to extend the range of his thinking virtually without limit, and to hold on to
it. Also he can develop a more complex organization of his meaning than is
open to him in talk – as complex as a poem or a play or a philosophic
dissertation. Having done so it is permanent, something which he can
come back to or which others can read without needing him there to expound it.

It has its place. But to understand it aright I should want finally to
merge the image of the writer in an image of the individual – as a person
committed to his own search for meaning, who has to interpret the flow
of events which happen to him and re-interpret in his own way the wisdom
and knowledge of others which lies outside him, as a person; who finds in
language an instrument at his disposal and in writing a way of using it.

Part One
Kinds of Writing

It is obvious that talk is intimately connected with social situations. Perhaps for some the situation is merely something to ignore in the interests of their own monologue. But we recognize such people as unusual. Ordinarily we expect talk to be a mutual exploration, topics to be held in common, communicants to be sensitive to each other – even if behind the official scenario they may be working on each other as well.

Since the writer writes alone, his situation is less obvious. Yet any writer must cope with situational factors which might have been otherwise. We can think of him as a diplomat negotiating between what is true to his topic, what is true to himself (or what of himself he wants to present), the requirements of his reader, and between the time, space and physical means he has available. The conjunction of all these will never be quite the same again.

Situations may limit what the writer can do or they may facilitate it. We should be chary of saying they define it. This would be to limit the capacity of the writer to interact with his situation. As well as conforming to the expectations he may bend them, resist them, act on them or otherwise escape from them imaginatively. Writing can seek an individual formulation which passes beyond the routine.

Equally, not all writing seeks this individuality – often with good reason. Reports in some contexts, minutes of meetings, instructions in telephone booths, receipts and invoices, some forms of business letter, jottings simply as reminders to one's memory – these would be examples where the writer has no need to pass beyond the formulaic. Involving nothing of himself in the writing, it may stand as if nobody wrote it. A similar procedure is sometimes adopted for political or theoretical writing. There perhaps it is more tactical.

Differences in situation, then, ensure that writing is of different kinds. The writer in meeting these situations has his experience of language use on which to draw. He will deal with his situation via the sorts of language use which seem to him appropriate to it. Writers have to develop their resources. A young child's topic on the Tower of London will draw on quite different resources of language from a sixth-former's 'essay' on a similar topic. Equally, mature writers on the same sort of theme may locate themselves in quite different areas of their resources. (Compare piece 2 in the following section, which draws on the resources of the spoken language, with piece 3, which draws on the language of formal Science.)

Finally, writings vary according to the general function of the language which they involve. Expressive writing remains close to the self. The writer presents himself as much as his matter to his reader and assumes a reader sufficiently close to enter with him into his purposes. Transactional writing involves a transition from this expressive matrix for the purposes of informing or persuading. Individual purposes and the presentation of self are subordinated to a matter which lies between the writer and his reader. We may inform, though, at many levels – recording, reporting, classifying and theorizing. Alternatively the writer may develop his expressive language towards a poetic construct.

In the pieces which follow something of this variety is documented. The reader may care to speculate about the balance between the situation the writer has had to meet and the way in which he has coped with it. Clearly there are different orders of difficulty involved. Consider particularly the matter of audience. It is clear that an audience remote in time or space is a difficult audience to engage compared with the known teacher who collects the books once a week, or the favourite uncle who lives round the corner. For part of what is involved in writing is anticipating what one can take for granted and knowing what one has to explain in detail. Pieces 1 and 11 in their different ways have sought and found a public audience, whilst 6 and 8 are much more private occasions.

He may like to think too about the resources of language on which each individual is drawing and about the tactics by which they achieve their objectives. There is the contrast between pieces 2 and 3. But what about the juxtapositions in piece 1 between personalized talk and formal psychological statement by which the audience is first wooed gently towards the writer's meaning and then dazzled by the apocalyptic close? There is the matter of style here too of course. Readers may like to reflect on the applicability of the scale developed by Martin Joos (frozen, formal, consultative, intimate, casual) (1961).

What too are the factors which underlie effective use of the different functions of language? Developmentally transactional writing must depend in some measure on the child's capacity to subordinate himself to the matter in hand. But then there is a range of ways in which the writer's sense of self can be integrated into the ongoing business that he has with his reader, or indeed that he has with himself as he writes his way towards a formulation which is satisfying. De-centring and re-integration might be one sort of process at work. It might also be worth reflecting on the different levels of generalization at work in different pieces.

We suggest two different orders of reading. (Two paths to a summit often give different views.) If one reads through from 1–11, one will start with a public statement and end with a public poem. That will be to cover the full range of purposes in one swoop. On the other hand, one might wish to speculate about how one kind of writing relates to another. We suggest, then, that one reads from 7–1 in that order, pausing for breath at 5 and 3; and then to read from 6–11, pausing for a moment after 8. If we think of 1 and 11 as flags flying on the top of a building to signify the maturity of a writer, then 6–8 are the foundations upon which that building rests.

1 Reality and Unreality in Education

When you were born, what was the first thing you experienced? You don't remember, which is a shame, for, as the Freudians tell us, our experiences in the earliest period of life dictate our characteristics in later life.

However, when you were born, it was likely that your first feeling was one of shock and horror at being ejected from your nice, warm comfortable womb, and being forced into the cold, antiseptic atmosphere of a hospital. The first sound a baby makes is a wail. I've never heard of a baby who laughed at birth.

Your next major experience was of your mother's breast. This brought back some reminders of the womb; it was warm, comfortable and a source of nourishment. And it was big – it gave you a place of refuge in the hard world. But after 6 months you were weaned. You were removed from your life-supply, and relatively left to fend for yourself.

But you still had your mother and your home. You could follow her around the kitchen, hold on to her ankles, and play with her most of the time. As well as this you began to become aware of another figure in your life – your father. The mysterious person who would magically appear at 6 o'clock every day, kiss your mother, kiss you and make himself at home. What did you feel about him? Was he mysterious, frightening, a threat, or a reassurance? Probably a mixture of all these, plus many others. But he was still part of a system which was recognisable – mother, father, home. You were safe. You were the centre of attention. When you cried you were fed, when you were wet your nappy was changed, when you had wind you were burped. Everything fitted into a fixed orderly pattern, with you in the centre.

Very little is known about how and what the infant perceives, and what is known is inconclusive. A few facts are certain: Firstly, the infant does not perceive in symbols, as the adult does. This means that when the baby sees a table, it is just that. It is not something which is brown, or has legs, or holds books in the air. It is all these things. It is one, a whole. Its size and shape and colour are not individual features, they are an integral part of the whole. Thus, the blue table in the corner is not the same as the red table in the middle of the room. They are two totally dissimilar things.

Secondly, an infant does not perceive the laws of cause and effect. If his ball rolls under the blue table, he won't crawl underneath to find it. He'll start crying. His ball has gone, vanished, because he can't see it any more.

But in due time he will be educated out of these fallacies. He will learn from experience, from his parents and then from his teachers what does happen to the ball. And this could be a good thing. An individual cannot survive in life without thinking symbolically, or without understanding the law of cause and effect.

Our entire educational system is based on the elaboration of these two tenets. We are taught to apply symbols to chemistry, physics, foreign languages, logic, philosophy, etc. We fit theories into symbols which are familiar and simple in order to understand what we don't really understand. The infant's world is one of true sensory experience. He loves his mother because she feels and tastes and smells nice. He likes his teddy bear because it's warm and furry. But how can we think in French, or experience the splitting of a chain of molecules? Through the media of education all experience is reduced to a set of second-hand symbols to be memorized and regurgitated at regular intervals.

Similarly with the cause and effect concept: In History, Economics, the Social Sciences and Mathematics, cause and effect are applied in immense complexity, from $1 + 1 = 2$, to integral calculus; from William of France + the Battle of Hastings = King William, to the intricacies of whether the Civil War was caused by economic, religious or constitutional factors. But, though many people know integral calculus, how many comprehend the 'Theory of Numbers'? Though most people can absorb an A-level History course, how many can feel the *urge* for democracy or the intensity of religious conviction?

Education, as we know it, is dealing in artificial and meaningless concepts. It is unreal in the sense that it has lost its point of contact with life. Scholars are so totally removed from actual everyday experience by the limitations of the examination system and the consequent necessity of picking others' equally meaningless symbolic experiences through the medium of the textbook, that all they can do is fill their minds with ever-increasing amounts of unreal, second-hand symbols.

The original innocence and purity of experience of the infant has been taken in hand, manipulated, altered and finally annihilated by the forces which say they 'educate' us. From youth, life has been subjected to a series of denials and rejections ... we have been fed into a machine which destroys our childhood experiences, by conditioning us to believe that childhood is somehow an inferior state and so invalidates any lessons we have learned then. 'You are not a child any more' – 'Grow up', 'you're being childish', 'You're acting like children' – these are now all terms of abuse, instead of being, as they should be, terms of praise.

As I have already said, all this type of education could be a good thing. It could be made acceptable by simultaneously encouraging the individual's development of his own mind – and by 'development' I do not mean an ability to store large amounts of data, or to think in the manner we now call logical. If kids were told, when they first started school, that what they would go through for the next fifteen or so years is basically rubbish, but is necessary, due to the present economic and political situation; and at the same time the child is encouraged to look *inside* himself, to explore his mind, and to re-affirm his earliest abilities of perception by whatever means possible; then, and only then, the system might be made just acceptable. But this is not done.

If it were true that it is necessary for the good of mankind as a whole, and the individual in particular, for our minds to be trained to think in artificial terms through the destruction of the child's natural mental state, even this would be excusable. But it is NOT.

The offspring of the educational system of the Western world has been the advanced technological state, and the characteristic of the advanced technological state is its high percentage of neurosis and psychosis, its tendency towards self-annihilation through the accumulation of its waste products aided by planned obsolescence, and finally its ability to destroy the whole of mankind and the planet through its ever-increasing proficiency in the manufacture and use of chemical, biological and nuclear weapons.

This is the result of education as we know it. No country bumpkin invented the H-bomb. It was the product of our primary, secondary and advanced schools of education, which have placed man in the hell of a mess he is in now.

*   *   *   *   *   *   *   *

'And you are sitting here listening to me speak, and we'll all go back to school tomorrow and learn history or chemistry or physics or something, and so it'll all proceed normally, until someone finally CRACKS, and then it'll stop.

For good.

And it won't be long.'

Danny *aged 17*

2 Atoms: The Chemical Bond:
The Plastic Washing-Up Bowl
Dedicated to the Dedicated Non-Scientist

Take a lump of coal, almost pure carbon. Take a knife. Divide the coal in two. Take one of the pieces. Halve that again. Continue the process. Eventually you will have to give up, either because you have decided that this game is too messy, or if you have a deeper interest in science and you are prepared to ignore the state of your hands, because the piece of coal is by now far too small to handle. In fact it is theoretically possible to proceed in this dissection process many thousand times more until the minutest particle which is physically and chemically identifiable as carbon remains. This is a carbon atom. Don't cut any further, else you'll split the atom and that isn't a good idea if you want to make a plastic washing-up bowl is it? A carbon atom is so small that millions of them are required for the full stop at the end of a printed sentence. All carbon atoms are exactly the same. It is absolutely impossible to distinguish between any two – they have the same mass (or weight), behave in exactly the same way and are therefore rather predictable, which is just as well if we want to start with carbon and finish with a plastic washing up-bowl, as it is useful to be able to apply the same process every day. One of the curious things about carbon atoms and about most other atoms come to that, is that they appear to behave as though they possess arms, four in the case of carbon, each terminating in an eager hand, ready to grab at some stray hand belonging to another atom, in order to satisfy their perpetual lust for security. Carbon is not only willing to hold hands with members of its own species, i.e. other carbon atoms, but also associates quite readily with members of different species e.g. hydrogen atoms (which unfortunately for them have only one hand restricting them to monogamy).

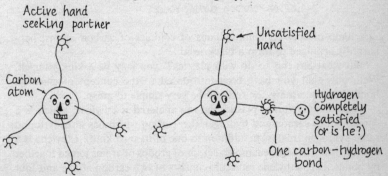

Active hand seeking partner

Carbon atom

Unsatisfied hand

Hydrogen completely satisfied (or is he?)

One carbon–hydrogen bond

Note the symmetrical position of the arms

What is more, if there are relatively few atoms available, one pair can take mutual comfort in holding hands twice, or even three times to give a double or triple bond respectively. Given the choice, though, the carbon atoms would prefer to hold hands with four different, or separate atoms, rather than waste three hands on the same fella (well, it's only natural, isn't it?).

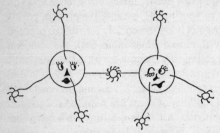

Carbon–carbon single bond

Note the stress

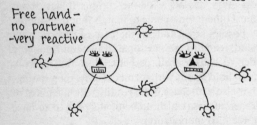

Free hand –
no partner
–very reactive

Carbon–carbon double bond

A lump of coal contains millions of colonies of carbon atoms, haphazardly arranged to form a black solid.

'But what has this to do with plastics?' you may be asking yourself. Well, now that you have been introduced to the concept of chemical bonds between atoms, the rest will be very simple to grasp.

When manufacturing plastic, the raw material is ethylene, which is a compound of carbon and hydrogen (i.e. carbon which has already found some hydrogen 'mates' in addition to one of its own kind). Ethylene is a gas consisting of identical molecules, or of groups of atoms joined together by bonds. Each ethylene molecule consists of two carbon atoms and four hydrogen atoms. It also contains a double bond.

Desperate unattached hand

Carbon-carbon triple bond
(the strain is almost killing them)

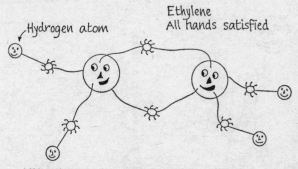

Hydrogen atom

Ethylene
All hands satisfied

All hands are well occupied with a companion so the molecule is a stable entity in this respect. But the two carbon atoms are under a small amount of strain due to the double bond. Having to bend their somewhat stiff arms around like this is really quite painful when they were made to point in a slightly different direction. The plastic manufacturer knows that if he treats the ethylene in a certain way he can break these double bonds and get one pair of hands to grab at a more comfortable situated appendage. So what he does is to crowd many ethylene molecules into a small space (i.e. he increases the pressure) with a dash of oxygen just to get things going. He then heats the gas to 200 degrees Centigrade and in the heat of the excitement, with the ethylene molecules wildly agitated, one pair of hands just have to let go – the strain is so great.

Well, as I explained before, carbon atoms are much happier to commit tetragamy than trigamy, as in the case of ethylene, therefore pairs of hands from different ethylene molecules link up readily; one hand grasps another molecule; that molecule's free hand then grabs another and so on, forming a huge chain of linked ethylene molecules. The resulting snake-like giant is called polyethylene, or **POLYTHENE.**

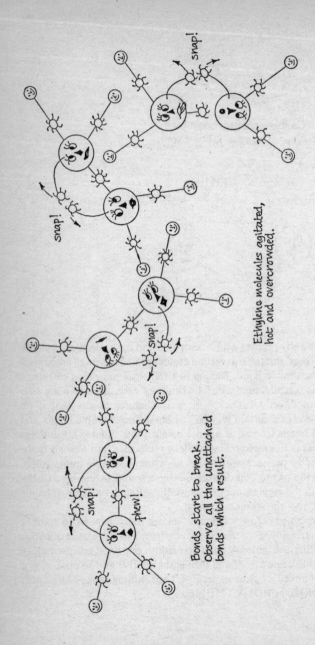

snap!

snap!

Ethylene molecules agitated,
hot and overcrowded.

snap!

Bonds start to break.
Observe all the unattached
bonds which result.

snap!

phew!

Part of a polythene molecule.

The molecule is too big to form part of a gas, in which the molecules must be light enough to fly around at great speed. What is more, these long winding molecules become entangled in one another to form a pliable solid PLASTIC. This then is your washing-up bowl material. Polythene is a thermoplastic, i.e. by heating it not too strongly it softens and can be moulded into the required shape.

There are many other types of plastic, but polythene is the easiest to understand.

Maryla *aged 17*
The diagrams have been copied from the original.

3

An organic compound $C_5H_8O_3$ turns blue litmus red and liberates carbon-dioxide from sodium carbonate. With ethyl alcohol and hydrogen chloride it forms a neutral substance $C_7H_{12}O_3$. It reacts with hydroxyl amine to give a compound $C_5H_9NO_3$ and with phenyl hydrazine to give $C_{11}H_{14}N_2O_2$. It gives the iodoform reaction with iodine and caustic soda. It is not affected by Fehling's solution or ammoniacal silver nitrate, but it is broken down by stronger oxidising agents. e.g. Nitric acid in two ways so that the products are partly acetic acid and maloric acid (a dibasic acid $C_3H_4O_4$) and partly carbon dioxide and succinic acid (a dibasic acid $C_4H_6O_4$). How many of the above reactions can you explain? Can you deduce the structure for the compound $C_5H_8O_3$?

From the formula of the compound, it could be a number of things. For example it could have acid groups, ketone groups, hydroxy groups, aldehyde groups and many others. Examination of the given properties of the substance limits these.

Since it turns blue litmus red, it could contain an acid group. This is borne out by the fact that it liberates carbon dioxide from sodium carbonate. This is a property of most organic or mineral acids.

$$2RCOOH + NO_2CO_3 \rightarrow CO_2\uparrow + 2RCOONa + H_2O.$$

where R is an alkyl (may be substituted) radicle.

The given substance reacts with ethyl alcohol and hydrochloric acid to form a neutral substance $C_7H_{12}O_3$. Any acid group will combine with an alcohol to form an ester with the elimination of a water molecule. Esters are neutral substances.

$$RCOOH + C_7H_5OH \overset{HCl}{\rightarrow} RCOO.C_2H_5 + H_2O.$$

R is equivalent to $[C_4H_7O]$. Bearing this in mind, the ester $RCOOC_2H_5$ has a formula $C_7H_{12}O_3$, which is in accordance with the given data. Since the substance will form esters, this is further evidence that it contains an acid COOH group. The hydrochloric acid acts as a catalyst in this reaction.

Aldehyde groups and ketone groups are the only common substances which will act with hydroxylamine and phenylhydrazine. Condensation products are formed and water is eliminated. Consider hydroxylamine. Any ketone or aldehyde will react to form an oxime.

$$\begin{matrix} R \\ R_1 \end{matrix} \!\!>\!\! C{=}O + H_2NOH \rightarrow \begin{matrix} R \\ R_1 \end{matrix} \!\!>\!\! C{=}NOH + H_2O$$
ketone.

$$RCHO + H_2NOH \rightarrow RC\overset{H}{=}NOH + H_2O$$

In the case of the aldehyde, if R is equivalent to $[C_4H_7O_2]$, the formula of the condensation product is $C_5H_9NO_3$. This is in accordance with the question.

Similarly, in the case of the ketone, $[R + R_1]$ must be equivalent to $[C_4H_8O_2]$, in which case the formula of the condensation product is still $C_5H_9NO_3$. Hence the given substance might also contain an aldehyde or ketone group.

Consider phenylhydrazine. With both aldehydes and ketones condensation products are again formed.

$$RCHO + C_6H_5MN.NH_2 \rightarrow R.CN.CH.C_6H_5 + H_2O$$

From before, if R is equivalent to $[C_4H_7O_2]$ then the condensation product has a formula of $C_{11}H_{14}N_2O_2$.

$$\frac{R}{R_1}{>}C{=}O + C_6H_5HN.NH_2 \rightarrow \frac{R}{R_1}{>}CN.NH.C_6H_5 + H_2O.$$

Similarly if $[R + R_1]$ is equivalent to $[C_4H_8O_2]$ the product of condensation also has a formula of $C_{11}H_{14}N_2O_2$.

This then only serves to confirm that the given substance might contain an aldehyde or ketone group.

Possible structures to the given substance:

I with an aldehyde group.

a)
```
      H  H  H  H
      |  |  |  |
O=C—C—C—C—COOH
      |  |  |
      H  H  H
```

b)
```
   H         H         H
   |         |         |
H—C———————C———————C—COOH
   |         |         |
   H    H—C=O      H
```

c)
```
   H  H  H
   |  |  |
H—C—C—C—COOH
   |  |  |
   H  H  C=O
         |
         H
```

d)
```
   H         H
   |         |
H—C———————C—COOH
   |         |
   H    H—C—H
             |
             C=O
             |
             H
```

e)
$$
\begin{array}{ccc}
\text{H}-\text{C} = & \text{O} \\
\text{H} \quad | & \text{H} \\
| & | & | \\
\text{H}-\text{C}-\text{C}-\text{C}-\text{H} \\
| & | & | \\
\text{H} & \text{COOH} & \text{H}
\end{array}
$$

II With a ketone group.

f)
$$
\begin{array}{c}
\text{CH}_3 \\
\text{C}=\text{O} \\
\text{CH}_3 \\
\text{CH} \\
\text{COOH}
\end{array}
$$

g)
$$
\begin{array}{c}
\text{CH}_3 \\
\text{C}=\text{O} \\
\text{CH}_2\text{CH}_2\text{COOH}.
\end{array}
$$

h)
$$
\begin{array}{c}
\text{CH}_3\text{CH}_2\text{CH}_2 \\
\text{C}=\text{O} \\
\text{COOH}.
\end{array}
$$

i)
$$
\begin{array}{c}
\text{CH}_3 \\
\text{CH} \\
\text{CH}_3 \quad \text{C}=\text{O} \\
\text{COOH}.
\end{array}
$$

The substance gives the iodoform reaction with iodine and caustic soda. The reaction only occurs with $CH_3C=O$ groups or substances which can be oxidised to this. Hence the structures a) c) d) h) and i) are ruled out. The reaction is as follows:

$$\underset{R}{\overset{CH_3}{>}}C=O + 3I_2 \rightarrow \underset{R}{\overset{CI_3}{>}}C=O + 3HI.$$

$$\underset{R}{\overset{CI_3}{>}}C=O + NaOH \rightarrow C.HI_3 + RCOONa.$$
$$\text{Iodoform}$$

the substance is not affected by Fehling's solution or ammoniacal silver nitrate. But aldehydes have reducing properties and would reduce ammoniacal silver nitrate to silver and form a red precipitate with Fehling's solution.

$$RCHO + NH_4OH \rightarrow RCOONH_4 + 2H^+ + 2e \Big\}$$
$$(Ag\downarrow \leftarrow Ag^+ + e)2$$

$$RCHO + H_2O \rightarrow RCOOH + 2H^+ + 2e \Big\}$$
$$(Cu^+\downarrow \leftarrow Cu^{++} + e)2$$

This shows that the substance must contain a ketone group and structures b) and d) are ruled out. Remaining structures are f) and g).

f)

$$\underset{\underset{COOH}{\overset{CH_3}{\underset{|}{CH}}}}{\overset{CH_3}{\underset{|}{\diagup}}}C=O$$

g)
$$\underset{CH_2.CH_2.COOH}{\overset{CH_3}{\diagdown}}C=O$$

Oxidation of the substance produces two sets of substances:

1) $[30] + C_5H_8O_3 \rightarrow CH_3COOH + H_2C\underset{COOH}{\overset{COOH}{<}}$

2) $[30] + C_5H_8O_3 \rightarrow CO_2 + CH_2COOH$
$$\qquad\qquad\qquad\qquad\qquad\qquad\quad | $$
$$\qquad\qquad\qquad\qquad\qquad\qquad\quad CH_2COOH.$$

consider structure g).

In order for acetic acid to be formed, an H atom must detach itself from the other branch so that the number of hydrogens is right, prior to oxidation.

$$CH_3$$
$$\searrow$$
$$\qquad C=O \qquad + [3O] \rightarrow CH_3COOH + COOH.CH_2.COOH$$
$$\nearrow$$
$$CH_2CH_2\ COOH$$

The substance left is maloric acid, which agrees with the question. If the same reaction is considered with structure f), acetic acid might be formed but the remaining hydrogens are in the wrong positions for maloric acid to be formed.

$$\qquad CH_3$$
$$\qquad\quad \searrow$$
$$CH_3 \qquad C=O \quad + [3O] \rightarrow CH_3COOH + ?$$
$$\quad \searrow \nearrow$$
$$\qquad C H$$
$$\qquad |$$
$$\qquad COOH$$

Hence structure f) is ruled out.

Therefore the structure of the initial substance is

$$CH_3$$
$$\searrow$$
$$\qquad C=O$$
$$\nearrow$$
$$CH_2.CH_2.COOH.$$

Jane *aged 17*

4 Australia in a Thimble

To sum up my work on Australia I have decided to put together all the general facts of Australia into one or two pages:—

Australia is a continent. It is completely in the Southern hemisphere. It is about one fourth smaller than Europe. It has a fairly rugged coast, with many inlets. It has one great gulf. This is the great Gulf of Carpentaria. It has one bight. This is the Great Australian Bight.

Australia is divided into seven states. They are:— Queensland, New South Wales, Victoria, South Australia, Western Australia, Northern Territory and Tasmania. The capital is Canberra. Australia's population is about 12,000,000 people.

The more common animals noted to live in Australia are the kangaroo family, the dingo and the duckbilled-platypus. Some birds are the cassowary and the emu and the ostrich. There is much desert in the centre of Australia especially in the Northern Territory. The largest range of mountains are in the east of the country. They are called the Eastern Highlands or the Great Divide. The largest river is the Murray which is 2,345 miles long.

The state capitals are:

Queensland   Brisbane
New South Wales   Sydney
Victoria   Melbourne
South Australia   Adelaide
Western Australia   Perth
Northern Territory Darwin

Australia has a warm climate without much rainfall.

Australia's industries are classed under five main headings. The industries are:

Pastoral   Sheep and cattle farming.
Agriculture   Wheat growing, fruit growing and sugar growing.
Mining   gold, copper, silver, lead, zinc and coal.
Manufacturing   iron and steel goods, leather articles, woollen textiles, soap and furniture.
Lumber   railway sleepers and road paving.

Australia is still a rising nation, which looks like having a wonderful future as a continent and a member of the commonwealth.

Jane *aged 12*

5 Driftwood

A rough piece of wood although smooth in places 6–8″ long. well grained especially along curves. Ugly looking knots which look soft although they are hard. Worn into the shap of a camels head or from another angle a dogs bone. 1 L bend. Coloured from cream shaded to dark brown dry and brittle from one end it could appear to be a fossil (nose end).

Zig zag cracks appear across the grains folation like marks under neck.

Girl *aged 18*

6 Driftwood reminds me:

Although only a piece of wood it has been worn away and broken down to such an extent that it forms the shape of a camels head. It is very old with loose sagging skin on its neck. It is a proud creature holding it head up high. The end of the piece of wood has been rounded this gives the shape of the mouth and the large knot on the angle of the wood forms the ear It could almost be a giraffe perhaps its the colouring that to me makes it like a camel on the sagging skin on its neck.

Turn the wood over and a new animal appears no longer gentle and docile but a snake with a large stareing eye. Its body has been cut in half and only the head section is left. It has pouched cheeks and a smooth body. It stands upright with its head high in the air. All it needs is a tongue.

Girl *aged 18*

7

The blood defences, it's called. And it's the defence idea I find most interesting, that and the organisation of it all. It's all so military, all of it, and so thoroughly practical. Think of the structure. Invaders appear – bacteria, intent upon their dirty work. Instantly, a signal to the defenders – but how? How do the phagocytes and lymphocytes *recognise* invasion? That's a question I'd like answered. Anyway, they do, somehow, in the mysterious, almost magical way the body has. And then, independent of brain directions, apparently, they move into action.

I like the subtlety of the methods of defence – but of the four, I'm most taken by the simple eating of the bacteria by the phagocytes. The slow, remorseless engulfing of the disease-carrier, while all around the mindless red cells continue their normal activities, completely undisturbed by the death-struggle going on among them – there's an epic quality about it.

In fact, now I've used the word 'epic' that's it. In this tiny sub-microscopic world, all the struggles of our 'real' world are taken to an ultimate degree of purposefulness. All the bacteria want to do is invade, kill, destroy: they have no high motives like 'defence of the fatherland'. All the phagocytes and lymphocytes want to do is to kill and destroy – the invader. And the battle-ground, with a stroke of divine appropriateness, becomes pus. Like the biblical thing of 'Out of the strong came forth sweetness' – but this time, for the health of the body, pus appears as a sign of health.

And while in one part of the body this terrible mammoth struggle for life is going on, the rest of the blood calmly continues its normal life, fetching, carrying, cleansing and purifying, just getting on with it. It makes me feel uplifted almost, as if it's some kind of Pilgrim's Progress allegory: O

Death, where is thy sting? O Germ, where is thy victory? I can almost *feel* the blood at work in my own body. It's as if I could focus down to see these extraordinary things happening a million times a minute all over my body. How odd.

Girl *aged 18*

8 Recollections

Monday evening. Me reading, my brother making an aeroplane. Phone rings and my mothers answered it. Cheerful hallo then her face all white and voice all wobbly. Put the phone down. Silence then – Ricky (my cousin aged nine) had been run over on this foggy November evening, his skull crushed, died in the ambulance.

We were all silent and incredulous. There had never been a death in our family. Incredible. My mother repeated it. We decided to go to my aunts house immediately leaving a message for my father to phone us – not saying what had happened.

We sat all that evening almost in silence. Nobody cried. Everyone was isolated in shock each sitting alone on his chair. Renee my aunt and Ricky's mother – Tom his father and Gloria and Stephen. I remember Renee kept saying – everyone must do as they feel best for them but somehow it was better to all just sit there. There was some comfort in the presence of all sharing this calamity. My memory of that evening is sharp – those pale faces strained but still. Kind of waiting – perhaps to wake up from a bad dream. Thoughts in my mind whirled, going backwards and forwards thinking about him, an ugly and precocious child. Precocious because we were all so much older than he.

The next morning I decided to go to school because there seemed no point in staying at home. I walked along the familiar back streets as if seeing them for the first time. These houses shops traffic lights I knew – never noticed but I saw them differently. They loomed – they were so solid – so inanimate. How could they remain unmoved when some bit of my life was shattered. Why were they the same when this had happened – but look so different as I stared out of the bony holes in my head. At school I had to meet my friends ordinary chatting. They did not know. I sat behind my desk lid not for once saying anything at all. After prayers I walked with a friend across the grounds. She was going to Biology – me to history. I told her and for the first time started to cry – it was hard to cry choking – not a release. She went. I sat on a seat until I stopped crying and finally went to my lesson. I must have been about half an hour late. The teacher said nothing. I wondered why. Usually one was asked. I sat always in the front row. It was about the 30 years war I think. I wrote notes mechanically in large scrawly writing not understanding a word. I do not know what that lesson was about. A year later when I came to revise my notes I could not read these pages, they made me feel sick. I tore them from the book and threw them away.

I don't remember much about the next few days. We – the children – that is, my brother cousins and I alternated between fits of hysterical laughing silence and irritability. I remember we read through all the letters of consolation and awarded each a certain amount of points – points being taken off for cliches like wherever he is he is happy now. These made me furiously angry for to me he was nowhere, finished. He had been but had gone out like a candle. We counted all the different euphemisms for death – passed away – gone before etc. etc. The fact that we did this so flippently filled me with guilt and I told everyone about it watching expectantly for the slightly horrified look on their faces.

The funeral was awful. The whole family squabbles about order in which people would go – does a second cousin go before a something in law. It seemed so incredibly mean and stupid. Wreathes and bouquets. One revolting woman had sent a wreath to Ricky from her dog. This nearly sent me crazy. It seemed like playing with this child's death. At best it was incredible sentimentality.

The service – For Jesus saith suffer the little ones to come to me – this smug stupid priest – how could he know how could he offer this drivel to these parents brothers and sisters. The grandfather made it worse by wailing and shouting. I should have died I've had my life – I'm an old man. He's only just begun. The coffin was so small and slid away behind the curtains.

What to do with the ashes. Everyone embarrassed – no idea – irrelevent but couldn't just let it go, O.K. scatter them on the rose beds at the crematorium. I went with them – the only one from my family. It was me who had read him stories – the cat who walked on his own. I can't remember it now but it had been Ricky's favorite. I went not wanting to but somehow supersitious – last respects – finally the end not more bustle and arrangements. Just reorganising life so the gap would not show.

We went to the crematorium scared as hell. Tense. Didn't know what to expect. A man in black came up to us carrying what looked like a giant salt cellar. Where do you want the ashes shaken? Rose beds? He didn't wait for stumbling explanations or questions. Quick as a flash he moved to the nearest bushes. Shake shake with the cellar. Good morning, a bow and was gone.

Silence. Incredulity. How ludicrous. Stephen laughed once. Stopped. Gloria smiled. Suddenly we three were doubled up laughing hysterically –

the sort of laughing that hurts your ribs, that dies down for a while then restarts bubble on bubble never to end.

We laughed for what seemed like hours absolutely uncontrollable, upsetting Tom and Renee though they understand we laughed from pain and agony, and non comprehension. This was death, this ignominious, ludicrous shaking a salt cellar. We had expected something tragic awe-inspiring. This insulted us totally and yet was a relief. It was so mundane – no mystery. A commercial transation. The man had many shakings to do in the morning – it was just a job. At least his attitude was straighter than the spurious comfort giving one of the vicer.

This was my first close acquaintance with death.

Judith *aged 20*

9 The Final Visit

The journey was long and tiring, and as the luxury coach continued, the winding country lanes, and swaying cornfields, which had at first been a joy to me, were making me dizzy with depression. The previous train journey had been bad enough, but this was even worse as it seemed I would never reach my destination – Wintleborough.

At last the bus turned into the small but pleasant village and it dropped me off outside a rather battered old post office . . . the street was deserted with the exception of a dowdy looking pensioner, who hobbled helplessly along the pebbled pavement. I didn't know which way to go . . . I couldn't remember where the 'home' was, as I had only visited it once before. I cautiously walked up to him and asked him if he knew, but he was deaf so it didn't help at all.

The wind whistled quickly down the narrow road, blowing away the debris left in the gutters. It was a Sunday and everyone was at home, eating their roast lamb and Yorkshire puddings and there was I out in the cold all on my own, wandering around. I was only eighteen at the time . . . not really old enough to understand life but one never understands it properly and even though I know this now, I thought then that I was the only person in the world who had troubles and miseries.

Finally, after walking around for an hour or so, I found a signpost pointing to the 'home'. At last I cheered up . . . I was happy and the thought of the prospect of being under a roof, was bliss. The rough pathway to the home was stony and uncomfortable as my thin soled shoes crunched over them . . . I now remembered my previous visit and as I saw the large authoritative building looming ahead of me I clearly memorised the day that I had been before . . . It had been hot, with a most beautiful sun in the deep blue sky but now it was winter and it was cold . . .

I marched through the frightening iron gates . . . I don't know why but 'iron wrought gates' give me the impression that any building with them is like a prison. I wasn't far wrong where this establishment was concerned . . . it was a miserable place.

I rang the bell at the entrance of the house, and the two large doors flung open soon after, bringing me face to face with a stern looking matron. I explained carefully to her about my business there and after a long ordeal she eventually remembered who I was. I was shown to a waiting room where I sat for quite a time. Nobody else seemed to be there and I felt a slight chill about the whole atmosphere. A grandfather clock stood in the corner of the room and every quarter of an hour it chimed in a low depressing tone. I watched every minute pass with slow industry and I became more and more nervous as the time ticked on.

At last I was collected by a beautiful nurse with the most lovely legs I have ever seen. I felt so sorry for her to be captured in such a career, especially in that old, outdated building. She took me quickly to a small dark room at the end of a corridor which was cold and poorly lit. Then she opened a door with a sign on it saying 'critical'. A man lay in a special bed, covered in blankets – he was my father, an old man with a haggered face, wild and glassy eyes deeply set under his eyebrows. Naturally he didn't recognise me, and I found it difficult to visualise him as the man I was brought up by, He had changed so much and he lay on his bed staring madly at the ceiling . . . I didn't know where to look – I had never seen a human being in such a mentally deficient state. His mouth lay agape and he kept making sucking noises with his tongue. When I enquired about him the nurse told me that he hadn't eaten for several hours – a certain sign of death . . . she seemed very concerned about him and I could see she was quite attached to him, after the many years of difficulty with him. I tried speaking to him, but he didn't even realise I was there, so after kissing him on the forehead and saying goodbye I left. The visit was short and sweet and I felt like leaving it that way. I had had enough for one day, so I entered the fresh air again and started my struggle back to the village. Before I was half way down the path, I heard a shout coming from the house and I saw the nurse running towards me.

I knew at once what had happened and as she broke the news to me my thoughts were far away. I didn't wait for more explanations . . . I just walked on, holding my head high and lifting my feet correctly. It all seemed so sudden and yet I was still to realise the true facts. Then, I thought it was only a dream, but now I know that it was my *last* visit. I ran into the wind.

Cathy *aged 18*

10 The Balloon Man

We were sitting in a row on the wall Sam, Belly, rog, Jap, Sal and me. All of us were kicking the wall and making clods of earth fly off it. We must have looked like a row of rheumatic Can Can girls.

'What shall we do?' asked Rog brightly (he was always the first one to ask this)

'Dunno,' murmured the rest of us.

There was a pause.

'Let's trail a policeman,' suggested Belly

'Always do that' murmured the rest of us.

Yet another pause.

'Let's go to the park' suggested Sam.

'Always do that' murmured the rest of us.

Only the thudding of our feet against the wall could be heard.

'Let's play mothers and fathers' suggsted Sal.

'Girls!' exclaimed the boys in disgust.

'Well that clearing in the woods is just right for a house' persisted Sal 'and all the bushes round could be the jungle and you could go hunting for food.'

'Yea! We could.' said Sam jumping off the wall and making a splat as he landed in a puddle. 'Let's catch ants.'

'Naw,' moaned Jap 'I wanna trail a policeman.'

'No. Let's do something different,' said I.

'It's alright for you to say that. You haven't thought of anything yet.' said Rog.

'Well I want to do something different.'

'Hey Sam,' yelled Jap, 'You got a flea on your back,' and Jap jumped off the wall onto Sam's back.

'Liar!' yelled Sam. 'You're the one with fleas. You got the Lurgy.'

'O.K. I'll give it to you.'

'Can't. I'm injected' said Sam clutching the top of his arm.

'Hey! Shut up and look over there!' I bellowed. They all looked in the direction of my pointing arm. Coming up the lane was a figure. We gaped at it. We had never seen anything like it before. It was a man. A very tall man in a coat that reached to his ankles. The coat was made from patches of materials in all colours and textures. He was walking or rather gliding very slowly towards us and above his head were hovering a multitude of balloons.

'Cor! Wot a funny bloke' giggled Jap.

'SSh' hissed the rest of us as if the slightest noise would disturb our consentration on the man. He was now nearly upon us and we could see his face. It was horrifying. It was a pea green colour and the veins in it shone out bright red. It looked as if the face was full of cracks. And his eyes. They were yellow like the sun but so much less friendly. But we felt no inclination to run, it was as if we were screwed down.

'Hello children' his voice was surprisingly thin and reedy. 'Would you like a balloon?' None of us made a move. 'Come, come surely you would each like one.' Again we made no move.

'You must take a ballon my innocents'

He was not at all emphatic but Sam put his hand out for a balloon. Then one by one the others did too. I felt my hand go out. Suddenly I really wanted a balloon. It seemed the most important thing in the world to me. He first gave balloons to the two boys standing on the ground. I was impatient. Then at last he gave one to each of us. I stared at the string in my hand and followed it up until my eyes alighted on the great green globe bobbing up and down above my head. I felt myself surging upwards, so too were the others. We were rising, very slowly at first and then faster and faster, until all that I could see was the balloon glowing white hot against the black sky. Then we seemed to slow down. I could see a young girl walking briskly across the blackness. A hand touched her on the shoulder. She spun around with a gasp. A huge evil looking man grabbed her around the waist with one hand and took her face in the other. He pressed his lips against hers. She struggled and kicked but she could not free herself. We looked on helplessly until a breeze carried us onward. After a while we again began to slow down. This time a group of men appeared in a ring. In the centre of the ring was another man who was different. We could not see what was different about him. We just sensed it. The eyes of the other man were filled with hatred. They produced long pins from nowhere and began thrusting them into the flesh of the middle man. He cried out but again we could do nothing, and were blown on.

Next we saw a man lying on his back quite motionless. His face beautifully calm. He looked perfectly happy but then we could hear weeping. A group of grey figures were coming towards him and weeping. They looked at him with dispair. They bent to touch him but as soon as they brought their fingers near his flesh they pulled them away in fear and wept harder. Why did they weep for one so happy? We had no time to find out. We were hurtling again through the dark void. We spun three times and there was an earsplitting bang above our heads. We were falling . . .

And then we were sitting on the wall exactly as before. It was as if the Balloon Man had never come. But then we looked at each other.

'Sam!' cried Jap 'You've got a beard . . .' Jap stopped dead. His voice was deep like that of a fully grown man. Again we looked at each other.

Sal's funny nose and freckles looked beautiful. And me, my spindly legs had thickened to support my new curvy body. Our clothes were strangling us. Our sleeves and trouser legs had crept up our limbs and when we moved there was a rending tear.

Why do we always portray Father Time as a broken old man in a white toga carrying a sythe, when we know he is not?

Karen *aged 13*

11 Someone, Somewhere is Shaking a Great Big Finger at You

How you kidded yourself that
You were daily threatened by the bomb
And really cared for napalmed babies
On the other side of the world.
Oh weren't you in, in, in,
Digging psychedelic noise and light
Every bloody Saturday night,
Making the break from putting on
The corduroys that mummy wanted
To going in jeans, who cares anyhow,
Man, you're an anarchist now;
It's not a philosophy it's a reputation:
Hitchhiking is in, so's paying the Tube fare
At the one-before-last-station.
And it's so difficult going through the process
Of growing a georgeharrison cum davygraham
Oriental Moustache
To fit in with the pot image.
And wasn't that a big farce too,
Getting high for five bob
Then puking up on the tube after.
Like some damn sozzled Irish navvy.
Then having to explain away
The puky smell on your dufflecoat,
To your dad, as the incompatability
Of beer and hotdogs.
And how you kidded yourself that
You were daily threatened by the bomb
As an excuse to indulge. Fullstop.
'Gather ye rosebuds' is the biggest
Excuse out.

When you're dead you'll still be made
Of the same stuff as me,
So what are you worrying about?
For Christ's sake will you stop probing
Into Undiscovered Tracts of Your
Snow-Bound Mind.
You might get a couple of thought-bergs
Drifting into ya' Id. KID.
You gotta live like death wasn't there.
Which means going blind for the rest of
Your life: Symbolically, that is.
But ya ain't got the guts
To do an OEdipus on ya eyes, or
A brutus on the Sunday joint carver.
So you gotta see the world
Through dozy coloured glasses, for all time.
Don't kid yerself you're really sorry
About anybody's death:—
MAN, you gotta be a Granite rock,
Wearing dozy glasses, smoking pot,
Wearing jeans, drinking napalm cocktails,
And really dying to live!

Christopher *aged 18*

Part Two
Sharing Experience

Much of the writing in our society is elaborate, complex and public. We have developed it to carry on our learning, our business, our government, our law. However, it is not even the written word which constitutes the child's predominant experience of language, let alone this form of it. Indeed nor can many of us remain in it for long. For child and adult alike it is in gossip and social interchange that the business of living is carried on; and what for the adult may be a point of welcome return is the point where the child begins.

Language which allows us to organize our picture of our experience allows us also to share it. So we fill our gossip with stories of what has happened to us, of the fruits of what we have learned. Thus the world is made aware of us and we of ourselves. Experience is shaped for our own pleasure and satisfaction even as we share it.

James Britton (1970) and D. W. Harding (1937) have developed the concept of the spectator role to deal with this side of our language use. In the spectator role we can take time off from the active business of our lives. Then we can work on our picture of the world and on ourselves, reconstituting the harmony by which we seek to live. The potentially damaging experience can be incorporated: the delightful one re-entered. Here we can evaluate and come to terms with the world in which we live.

Much of the time we do this informally, even privately in our own heads or with a few close friends. Yet there are more developed ways. An anecdote can be worked on till it becomes a short story. The undeveloped 'I' of informal narration may become the developed fictional or autobiographical character. A mood or a feeling may become a poem. Form allows a more complex organization. Just as our musings may shuttle between the real and imagined so we may use form to enter actual or possible or fantastically impossible experiences. Autobiography, fiction or fantasy are perhaps no more than the developed forms which make clear to the reader which is which.

In the section which follows it is this direction which we document. The reader may care to speculate on the processes by which the writer is enabled to achieve his final balance between raw experience and artistic form. Birth and life are assimilated for example in Monica's story 'The Duck Family' (piece 2), yet for the six year old the account remains particular and its symbolic force unfocused. By contrast Tony's 'Tube Train Trauma' (piece 17) seems to concentrate the evaluation of a whole world in the regularity of a current event.

It may be of interest too to reflect on the nature of the experiences which the writing seeks to harmonize and to celebrate. For it is not the same world for six or sixteen year old, for girl or boy, for you or me. We each have our individual fears and delights. Yet what underlies the fascination of fantasy for the young child with its recurrent polarities of the grotesque and the beautiful, of the world displaced and the world assured? Why is experience so often located for the adolescent in the form of the solitary meditational musing? There are regularities of emotional development which bear examination. If we had had the space it might have been most interesting to have followed a single individual's writings in this direction over a year.

Perhaps, too, one may wonder why it is that young children seem to develop their understanding of the purposes implicit in the poetic function of language so much earlier than their understanding of the transactional – at any rate in developed form. Is it simply that they encounter the stories which are read to them at an earlier age? Art's patterns of tension and release may chime much more immediately with a child's early sensing of regularity in the world.

Here are three pieces of writing from primary school. Caroline, in sifting the events of her week, discovers and focuses on the occasion which interested her most. Monica and Genevieve sat together and talked about their duck stories while they wrote them; the experience was shared, and traces of this remain in what have become their individual stories. Susan is conscious of 'telling a story', mingling the fictional forms she has met with the familiarities of her own everyday life.

1

on wensday I went to my Nannys   on Thesday we went to London and we had diner in St James Park then we went to the pictures and I saw a film of anne blolin   before we went into the pictures I bought a doll and it was called catherina of aragon   She has a pink dresse on   then we went home. The next day we went to a common   on saterday we went to a sorp [shop] in the norning roned the coner from were my nanny lives.   in the afternoon we went two the pictures agene   at first we saw a cowboy film then we saw a film called the hundred and one dalmations   it was about a hundred dogs   at first there were ownly 15 and they all lived in a little house with there mother and there father.   one night when there owner had takon there mother and father out two men came and stole them   there was a lady who wontid them two   the two men took them home and they saw more dogs   then a cat begaen two try two get them out but he codent so it was feney [funny] becaes the cat kepped on knocking things over   so the two men saw him and they got very cross with him   they were silly the lady who wanted them all was very silly   she had a very funny fase and she got very cross with the two men.   the two men were funey two and evrything they were going two do it always wong.   the cat who was still trying two get the hundred and one dogs out   he made a hole in the wall and then traed to get them allout   he Got out the hundred and one but he codent   but soon he did and they all got home so they lived happy ever affter.

Caroline *aged 6*

2 The Duck Family

One day there was a mother duck and a father duck   They did not have a duckling. She wished she had a baby duckling but one day she had a bad pane and father duck thought that she was going to have a baby   When mother duck hurd what father duck had said mother duck said I hope what you thought is trouw   They stated looking for things to bild the house so they could have a baby. In a week she was siting on her egg   in

a nother week The egg was craked and out came a littlr brown baby   They
gave him a lot of food and the baby was very happy all his life.

Monica *aged 6*

3 The Duck Family

one day ther was a daddy duck and a mummy duck they livd togther in a
Pound   one day mummy duck didet feele very well so daddy duck sat
douwn on a lef and thot sudney he thot she was going to have a baby   so
he ruche ofer to Mummy duck   so she thot – so she watit for a long time
of all off a sudern she had a little duck.

Genevieve *aged 6*

Susan wrote this story spontaneously and unaided during a holiday at home.

4 Susan's Story

Chapter 1 The three Wishes

Once upon a time, the was a very wicked witch Called Ibbleobleookface
she was called this very funny name because she could change to any
unhuman face she wanted to change into. One day she made a special rule
that anybody who could kill the three trolls up at the top of a mountain
could have three wishes   many poeple tried but they just got killed
sent back to the witch of course by slaves because they were dead.

Chapter 2 The Prince

One day a prince from Wales came to try his luck   the witch made him
wait a few days till it was very cold and dismal   she made him set off at
night as well witch made it worse. At last he came to a great mountain
with fire on top   would that be the fire of the trolls or fire of a volcanoe
he climed the mountain but it was a volcanoe

Chapter 3 The volcaneo – The 1st wish

Now when he climbed down the Volcaneo he came to a mountain with
grunting and talking coming from the top and there was fire   so he
climbedthat when he got too the top guess what he saw . . . . . . the trolls
grunting to each other   he had behind a rock and listened to them   he
couldnot understand what they were grunting about   they were going
htnysayh He took his gun out and shot the first troll   then he took a
bow and arrow and threw it at the troll   bang the troll fell down dead
now in the woods near to the wictchs castle there lived a magic fairy   now
this fairy loved young Princes very much   she could see the prince on top

of the mountain she waved her wand and the 3rd troll fell down dead then he thanked whoever it was and made his way back to the castle.

Chapter 4 The next task

Ow dear Im tired said the prince when he got back now for the next task said the witch to the prince ow no ow yes said the witch to him the prince went red in the face and said WHAT You can go and kill three tigers bring them back when you have done so now go on be back before the sunsets at these words the prince ran though the woods but he did not spy any tigers he only saw little things like rabbits squirrels he shot a few rabbits that the witch might like he slept in the woods for a few nights and then he made his way to the Jungle.

Chapter 5 The sunset

When he got to the Jungle the sun was getting ready to set. He dident have much time now so he ran along the path and then he herd a growl and then it was loudar and then up came a tiger he took out his gun and shot BANG he shot the first tiger now he had two more tigers too shoot then he saw some stripes in the darkness (I say darkness because the sun set late that night) He crept up to it and shot Bang the gun shot the tiger fell down dead one more to catch the sun had nealy go in he though he could turn back now.

Chapter 6 The very last tiger

So he turned back and he managed to catch the last tiger (I canot tell you how it would take a very long time) but anyhow he caught it he had to run back to the witch so he turned back he had to run back because the sun was allmost setting he dashed back to and said to the witch I SHALL NOT DO ANYMORE all right said the witch you may have youy wishes

Chapter 7 The Wishes

So the witch gave the prince the wishes the prince said thank you shall I tell you what the wishes were

1. that he became King
2. he could live in a castle
3. he could be the richest man in a the kingdom.

T H E

H   N

E N D

Susan *aged 7½*

With the increase of self-consciousness there develops the possibility of using writing as a means of looking at oneself reflectively; the writer begins to realize and examine some personal concerns. An imaginative comparison between the sound of his blown nose and a French horn leads Daniel to comment with a witty detachment on his slow progress at music. For Stephen, his reflection becomes an alternative personality not entirely unlike himself. Kevin's poem shows a developing ability to inquire into the self by means of symbols, while Robert is not simply remembering an event but examining his recollections.

5 My Face

I stood in fornt of the mirror and stared, the eyes in my refection stared and stared. I counted the ripples on my forehead when I frowned, and tried to count my spots. I wrincled my nose and pulled my hair down to see how I looked, I couldn't see, my hair is too thick and dirty. My hair covered my eyes and I sucked strands as they reached my mouth, they were taste-less and I spat them out; they clung wet on my cheek and I brush them behind my ear. I sniffed and had to blow my nose, the noise echoed in my room, and it reminded me of my failing attempts at the french horn in Music. My sore lips hurt and I scratched them. I winced but the pain had gone as soon as it had come. My white cheek usually red was pale, I rubbed it red, then back to white.

Daniel *aged 12*

6

When I look in the mirror in the morning I see a face which seems to say 'Why do we have to get up so early in the morning?' and then it sort of fades away and is replaced by a much happier sort of face. He must be a sort of personal body-guard or servant because he is there whenever I look. He may be a sort of king who is always looking after his followers and who doesn't listen when you talk to him for whenever you are talking so is he and he never says anything unless you do. A bit of a queer really what with his crown of tousled hair and sleepy eyes.

At other times of the day he is just a ghost to whom I pay no attention at all but in the evening he is there again, just a black figure in the darkness just waiting for me to wake up again in the morning. It must be awfully boring to be king, ruling over one person, just an image whom you can never touch and who exists in all shiny objects.

Stephen Berry *aged 13*

7 I have . . .

I have an eagle in me,
Picking at my brain,
As if picking a worm,
Out of the ground,
Day and night,
It stretches and pulls my head,
Tearing my brain apart.

I have a heart in me,
Living but waiting for a
Chance to kill!
And be rid of me,
It lives for envy.
Gradually it is taking me over,
Its a menace to my system.

I have a tiger in me
Leaping and roaring inside
Making me writhe
In agony!
It snarls at me,
Shaking my ribs and sides,
It just roams around.

Kevin *aged 12*

8 Show-Off

I wish I had a new dress,
Its her very best,
Its orange with a big thick belt,
I wish I had a new dress.

She shows off in her new dress,
I would not I think,
I hope I do not,
I wish I had a new dress.

She walks down the road making the boys look at her.
I wish they would look at me,
I would not make the boys look at me,
'Oh' she shows off in that dress.

She's got an orange handbag to go with her dress
And orange shoes,
She's got an orange hair-band
'Oh' she shows off.
I wish I had all the things she's got.

Kim *aged 12*

9

When I was small I used to be fond of climbing trees. A tree that I was particularly fond of was an old gnarled apple tree at the bottom of my garden. Usually on Friday afternoons I would climb to the highest branches and scan the horizon which was broken by Church spires, houses and trees. I think that I used to enjoy this experience because subconsciously I could sense the week was over and that tomorrow (Saturday) was a day of rest.

Robert *aged 13*

In the following pieces there is a continued concern with writing to explore areas of experience. There is also a developing enjoyment in the possibilities of discovering something when we write about it. Tony, Annabel and Miranda in their different ways all draw deeply on their resources to create the verbal sense of something there. Formulation is pursued, even hunted, until it is adequate to represent the power of the experience.

10

Place shaking thundering down on the victorious Gunners, shouting out we are the champions so f*** all the rest. Pelting with rain like a soggy sponge, wet right through to the skin, clapping our hands and hoping to win the Fairs Cup. Bloody coppers in the way, pull you out for doing f*** all. The referee's a c*** we chant, for giving decisions the other way, bloody East Germans all the same these ruddy foreigners. Number one goes in, the stadium's in an uproar, like the world has just exploded. Tears falling everywhere, just one more bloody goal needed and we will have won. And the shouts go louder and louder

for we want two we want two. Half time came, lucky bleeders survived, you wait till the second half, and we'll knock the pants off them. Reds come out up goes a shout we want two we want two, we are the champions of Europe a voice says. We need two goals. Suddenly the ball enters the net, we've scored again, everybody pushing and shoving me, but I don't mind, we are the champions, we are the champions so f*** all the rest. The place is in an uproar people lying on the floor half dead with gladness to see our team win. Seconds later another goes in oh why what a great team, what a great team we've got. Banners on

my head, crashing like thunder, sky is red and joy for all Arsenal supporters. Guns roar loud, bloody sirens it's those foreigners again like amateurs in a nursery school. We are the Arsenal and we are the best, we are the Arsenal so f*** all the rest. E for B and Charlie George they chanted, and then came 'you'll never walk alone', this was a sign for all Arsenal supporters to raise their scarves, it was like red sky at night. Then everybody jumped up and down to knees up Mother Brown, oh why what a rotten song, what a rotten singer to . . . . . .o. The whistle goes oh what a roar, the players are crying, jumping

for joy, we receive the trophy, it's raised by our skipper, you'll never hear a louder cheer in your whole life if you were at this game. ARSENAL, ARSENAL, ARSENAL, ARSENAL, ARSENAL, ARSENAL, ARSENAL, A-R-S-E-N-A-L, ARSENAL, ARSENAL, ARSEN-AL, we are the greatest, and we chant we are the Victorious. The shine shone on this magnificent trophy from the floodlights, it was great rejoicing evening for all red and white supporters. People were drunk getting picked by coppers, but they don't care they have won the cup. We are the champions, OH ARSENAL, OH ARSENAL, WE ARE the Champions. Coppers lost control and thousands invade on to the pitch just like changed beings of an invisible race, like prehistoric mummies in a smaller way, what a fantastic feeling to erupt on a night like this.

Tony *aged 15*

11 Starlings

I found them shivering with cold huddled to each other ready to die in the cold of the night or warmth of a dog's jaws. Two little starlings deserted by their mother and dropped from a nest in the roof of a barn, and hurled to straw covered floor. Thin, bony, shaking and squawking in the midst of a rat infested floor. Poor, dependent living things needing food, warmth and security that they had left seven hours before.

Their fate was to die as others have and will, but I suddenly wanted to pick them out of the dirty floor and feed them and hope that they would live. I dared not pick them up in case they would fall to pieces, but I scooped them up in my cupped hands taking some straw as well. I slowly made my way back to the farm house, scared of dropping them but also squirming slightly at their moving about in my hands. Gradually a small crowd of children came to admire them. I got inside the house and found a cardboard box to put them in. I covered it in more straw and endeavoured to pick them up. They had no feathers and their bones were covered loosely with pink baggy flesh with goose pimples all over. I put my hands around one and felt the cold lumpy flesh and the spikey framework underneath. I shivered at first and then managed to get a soft grip on its ribs on either side of its back. I put it into the straw in the box and hurriedly took my fingers off that slightly sticky surface. Then I looked at the other, stark, pink and ugly needing food. I tenderly wrapped my hands over its back and ribs and picked it up quickly and placed it in the box – quickly. They were very weak but they still managed to scream for food. I took the box into the kitchen and put it on the table the centre of attraction. As I was at riding school, I could not help myself to the food for the starlings. So I had to ask and I was not refused.

I busied myself about the kitchen, making mixtures of mashed up boiled egg and bread and milk. I sat on a stool round the table and proceeded to feed them. By this time they were making a dreadfull noise and I had to feed them quickly. I dipped my little finger into the egg and put it down the throat of one. Their bright yellow beaks were wide open waiting for fat juicy worms to be put into their mouths. I got used to feeding them with my fingers and they got used to me. Their eyes were not open yet so they presumed me to be their mother.

Days went by. Every morning, afternoon and night I poured buckets of water over soil and dug for worms. Still their shrieking did not cease. They got stronger, less sticky and knew if you were there or not. I was fascinated by them by now and would have been heartbroken if they had died. Everyone admired them and I was working like a slave preparing their food and stuffing it down their huge throats.

Then my parents came to collect me. I pleaded and begged to take them home and I was allowed to. We bought on the way home a huge packet of mealy worms for the birds to get through in the car.

They got stronger and their eyes had opened. One was getting very intelligent, like plucking at moving things. This one we called Charlie. Charlie learnt to fly but the other one did not manage to. They had beautiful grey downy feathers and their beaks did not look so large.

I started letting them free in the garden. I taught them to catch wood lice and pick up worms. But all this time the weak one was making no progress. Charlie flew away and never came back. He had been longing to go and was very strong and intelligent. I missed him and was very sad that he went. The next day the other one was very weak. After school she was lieing on her tummy and we gave her some brandy to revive her, but she died.

I have learnt a great deal from these starlings

Annabel *aged 13*

12 Worms

Kicking the dry leaves
Searching the grass for
Minute mountains of upturned earth,
This was our pastime in
Autumn days.

Approaching these minute snakes
We prodded and poked them
So that the creatures broke
Apart, so both ends
Slithered back and disappeared
Into the dark
Enfolding earth.

Mating worms,
Their bodies glued together
By a long, white
Squelchy cord
Which pulsated as I ran
My finger along the flesh
Which oozed
A slimy liquid.

The loathsome sight
Of worms mating
Was repugnant,
Yet my instinct and desire
Urged me to continue,
To feel the slime
And pulsating beneath my finger,
And the sight of parting worms.

Miranda *aged 13*

13 Making Someone Cry

We were bored. It was an hour before tea time and we'd run out of things
to do. We were a group of ordinary twelve year olds, and so we always
got bored quickly.

I was just trying to kick a small stone up from the road and onto the
pavement when I saw a small skinny boy walking towards us.

'Come on', I said, 'let's have some fun.'

We all ran towards the boy, who hesitated when he saw us coming.

'Hello Jimmy,' I said cheerfully 'how's your dad today? Got enough booze has he? We wouldn't want him to go without.'

He walked around us without saying a word. We walked after him.

'He got up early this morning, didn't he?' I continued. 'I saw him getting up as I walked home from school at me dinner hour, that's how I know.'

'But that must have been as early as 12.30,' chipped in another boy.

'He'll be going to Sunday School next,' said another. The boy increased his pace and we increased it with him.

'Don't run away Jimmy', I said 'you'll make us feel unwanted.'

'Oh go away can't you!' he said, 'go and start on someone else for a change.'

'We're only trying to cheer you up, we're doing our best. I tell you what, we'll all chip in and give your dad another bottle. We couldn't do more than that.'

'I'm getting sick of this, every day you get at my dad. You . . .'

'Temper, temper; we're only trying to help, we keep telling you.'

'It's not his fault, he can't help it. He's been unlucky.'

'Leave him alone,' said one of the boys.

'You know,' I continued, taking no notice, 'I'm sure I saw your dad with that pro in Giler street.'

Jimmy looked at me with hate in his eyes. Slowly tears slid down his face. He said nothing, then turned and burst into tears.

We turned and walked off. I was grinning, but when I looked around the other kids were looking at me in a funny manner.

'Come on', I said, 'I was only having some fun.'

Ronald *aged 14*

14 Out of Reach

Very few people really enjoy practising a musical instrument for any length of time. I suppose there must be a few who do it willingly or there would not be any brilliant young musicians; I am not one of these exceptions and my reasons for particularly disliking doing practice on my cello are perhaps not the usual ones.

My sister is a lot older than I am and for as long as I can remember she has played two instruments, as it seemed to me, quite as well as is heard on the radio. To some people, I am sure, this would have been an encouragement but on me it had the reverse effect. There is always some music going on in our house and when I was quite small I felt quite sure I should be expected to play something myself, so that when a half-size cello was discovered almost by accident, it seemed to everybody the obvious solution.

I was eight at the time and small though the cello was, it seemed enormous to me and I approached it with mixed feelings. In a way I was quite keen to conform to the family pattern but when I heard the horrible sounds I made my heart sank. Everybody encouraged me, and my sister, who as sisters go is quite tolerant, often tried to help me, and played my accompaniments for exams etc. But the house is often full of professional-sounding string players and I am quite sure that however regularly I practise I shall never be able to make sounds like they do. On these occasions I have a tendency to hide away, certainly I put my cello out of sight, lest any of these well-meaning friends should ask me to play and give me more encouragement.

The one thing that puts me off enjoying playing the cello is the fact that my sister and her friends are so much better musicians than I could ever be; and if my sister is about when I am practising I feel sure she must be thinking how terrible it is. It is not that I do not like music. I really quite enjoy going to concerts and I even do not mind singing in moderation. Occasionally I am persuaded to play in children's orchestras and there, where I cannot really be heard (or so I believe), like Sparky and his magic piano, I get a brief glimpse into the musicians' world. Just occasionally when I am practising the cello I find that I have momentarily succeeded in producing a sort of sound that should be made, and then I am back to the scraping and squeaking which I so dislike and which makes me realize that what I am aspiring to is, for me, out of reach.

Philip *aged 13*

When he has completed his work, the writer's feeling of success may approximate to the pleasures a craftsman feels when he has achieved an exactness. He may assume a position of detachment from which he looks at the material he has given life to and gains satisfaction from its individual form. The casual, random progress of Tony's 'Tube Train Trauma' is conscious; he knows he is holding the camera, and his effects are judged. Though there is no regular rhyme scheme in the poem, the reader is nudged forwards to the shock four-letter word by a preceding rhyme, or, to take another example, the phrase 'London Transport provide all the thrills' presents simultaneously a knowing comment and a parody of a publicity handout. The writer is aware of what he is doing, and enjoying his sense of control.

The child at any age may range between a free flow of ideas and a highly organized composition; Daniel, for example, can write 'The Albatross' within a relatively short space of time. The older child, however, is increasingly in a position to make a conscious choice from the resources available to him.

15

One crumb to feed a million,
the rest to feed a few.
Work, you millions, for your crumb.
    24 hours a day.
Work while your boss eats
tons of food a day,
and leaves much more for the pig.
    Envy the pig.
The bosses can't eat everything.
So put it in the sea,
    burn it.
Don't let the slaves get strong,
or they will put us down.
If we make them starve,
they will pay more for their food.
    Money,
    the reason for all this,
    as if you didn't know.
And the names of the bosses,
    Religion, Business, Government.

Anon *aged 14*

16 The Albatross

I've got an albatross in me,
A lonely albatross, a wandering albatross.
A swooping cavorting albatross,
An albatross so wild he tears me in half.
An albatross that dives and banks in his endless
    search for food.
I've got an albatross in me,
An albatross so sleek and graceful.
An albatross so fast and swift,
An albatross that curves and banks in the
    wave swept wind.
I've got an albatross in me,
An albatross that plummets in ever decreasing
    circles.
An albatross that skims for years through curling
    waves and hydrophonic winds.

An albatross streaked black and grey by
   harmonic winds and waves.
An albatross that nears its end in screeching
   winds and echoing waves.
An albatross that will face its death on
   splintering rocks and whirlpool waves.

Daniel *aged 13*

17 Tube Train Trauma

Metal redworm,
Commutes bowlers and brollies
From suburbia to city.
Then back at night.
Transports fag-ends and beer
Cans, passengers
Near to insanity.
Without book or newspaper,
You read the car-cards.
Lacking a companion
You rape with your eyes
And resist the temptation
To pull the communication
Cord. Play games.
If the train got stuck
Suddenly, for weeks on end,
Which girl would you fuck
First, assuming she'd let you?
Try reading the minds
Of people who stare
At you like you had spots.
Open flies. Or could it
Possibly be the length
Of your hair that bothers them?
You try to ignore
The bundles of rags, curled
In the corners of seats.
But as long as they snore
Or you see that they're breathing,
You're sure they'll end up all right.
Avoid braces and boots,
Empty carriages and anyone

Seeming the type who
Shoots and asks questions later.
It can be fun on the tube,
Without doubt. Then you step,
Suddenly, in the depths of a tunnel,
And then all the lights go out.
London Transport provides all the thrills.
Quick service from civil-war uniforms.
Robbing you all with a smile.

Tony *aged 17*

18 Writing

I enjoy writing most of all the things I do. I draw, play the piano, I read and many other things but writing is the one that I can express myself best in the way of different words and statements. When I am writing my mind is talking to me, mentioning ideas and at the same time calculating where to put a certain statement and try to build a foundation for my essay. I try to let nothing escape me which would enable the reader to understand more clearly what I was describing or explaining. Whenever I write my mind is working too quickly for my hand to put my thoughts into words on the page, so I very often miss out things which I would have preferred to stay as a concrete slab firmly in the foundation. I spend about twice as much time on one sentence when writing it than when I am speaking it. I may elaborate on words, lengthen the sentence, add on a few words that I might forget whilst talking. The main things that I correct when I write down something are, the slang I use whilst talking, the repetitiveness I have when I talk, the exaggeration I make when I talk, and the way round I put my words in a sentence, which always get muddled up when I'm desperately telling someone something.

When I talk I describe nearly everything with my facial expressions, my hands and my movements. I find myself exaggerating a lot, for instance I say 'miles' for an inch or yard, and 'millions' for about three of something, but though I do do that people catch on in a second because they follow my expressions and understand the story I am telling them before I start. When one is talking, one is not taken literally because everyone exaggerates. For instance someone might state, having just arrived from a tropical country 'Oh it was absolutely awful. Thousands of horrid red ants crawled all over me.' But that would not be strictly true because the man who said this would have been dead by now. But people accept that the number was not thousands and perhaps was three or four. When one is talking one does not exaggerate meaning to tell an untruth, but to make one's point clear, for instance if someone had to wait for his girl friend at 10 o'clock for an hour, he might say 'I've been waiting for hours and hours.' but only to emphasise his point of having to wait.

When one is talking one doesn't have to set out the plot or foundation first and then lead up to what happened because one can express what you want to say in a shake of the hand or jerk of the elbow. But nothing is more annoying than trying to follow someone talking or writing about something that is not carefully planned out, for instance my old English text book at my primary school used to ask, 'Mr Fletcher has five cousins and two neices and nephews being twins, having two uncles being father to the cousins, how many daughters has he got?'

I prefer writing to talking because it is somehow a calmer atmosphere – you are not snatching and grasping for words, and having only two minutes until people get disinterested in what you are saying. There is much more scope in writing, one has time to search for words to put in the appropriate place, wheras when one is talking one has to be content with a word that doesn't do. One has a better chance when writing to prove a point with words but not with expression. That is why politicians prepare speeches, so they can have the right thought out statement in it, and, at the time of the speech, also the expression.

The writing I prefer doing is using mostly historical facts and putting in my imagination, which when put together well makes a lovely story. I feel secure in a story based on historical facts which are great fun to embroider on. The recently televised 'Six Wives of Henry VIII' and 'Elizabeth R' are my idea of a dream, spending hours on the murder scenes and minutes on the political business. But I do enjoy imaginative essays, in fact I like the happy medium best. I do a lot of writing for myself, but always I have an awareness that someone someday will read it, and I don't know why but it slightly inhibits me. I enjoy writng for school, but I do like the freedom of wiping out the vision of someone else reading it which makkes me very aware of what I am writing. My writing changes quite a lot depending on who is about to read it. I feel myself bending towards the type of thing I think the reader likes – always to suit them. I actually think now that I may sway because I have the thoughts of what mark I might get if I write what they like.

At my primary school every teacher had his or her pet type of poem or story. Mrs. Bell had to have ones about the seasons, Mrs. Hardy had to have rhyming ones and so on. We practically reproduced ther 'ideal' poem every time we wrote for them. We had no freedom of thought whatsoever.

It is very difficult to know what people like, want and understand. For instance in a story I might write something very wierd with an inner meaning especially for the reader, and the reader does not understand it; or I might think I had hit upon the very thing the reader wanted and it misses the point in the readers view. But people's minds are very different and view things in different ways, so in order to make sure the reader or audience understands, you have to adapt to the reader's Ideas.

Whilst writing this it has become apparent to me that one pays much more care and attention to what one writes than what one says. Misunderstandings between people arise because they have not so much care as there should be, it would help the communication of people today if they paid more attention and real care to their speech.

Annabel *aged 13*

Part Three
Handling Information

The previous section attempted to document something of the continuity between gossip and art. But just as the written word enables the anecdotes of informal talk to be translated into the complexity of a finished poetic organization, so also it increases our power to inform or to persuade. This is the area of our discourse where we deal with the objective world. Generalization and abstraction give us power to act.

Despite the value which we attach to art it is round the informative and persuasive uses of language that society has gathered its resources. Here is enshrined the knowledge which gives us wealth, which offers us control and understanding of our environment. Language in this area is highly developed in consequence. Somewhat formidably, then, the public modes of discourse within the various communities (academic, business, legal, political) confront the developing writer.

Removed from this public context we can handle information in various ways. Much of the dealings of young writers may be merely with thinking it through. They, like anyone who meets with a new idea, have to get the feel of it, throw it around, mull it over – all to make it fit with an existing picture of how things are; sometimes too, to modify that existing picture before the new information can fit at all – a modification that may take some considerable time. It is for this reason that we talk things over; but the written word can serve the same purpose.

Setting down an account for someone else involves the passage from the attempt to assimilate the idea for oneself to the attempt to locate it in someone else's understanding. Here the writer has to engage with his reader – to anticipate what he can take for granted, to know what he must explain in detail. He has to negotiate his route. He will have to modify his style and his tactics accordingly.

Much of the public writing of the academic disciplines operates at a high level of abstraction. However much the writing may be embedded in exemplification, it is, by and large, theoretical information which it serves to advance. Such uses do not exhaust the level at which it is possible to inform. Reports of what has happened, classification of particulars beneath generalizations are examples of other levels. They are often useful in the process of learning in school. Equally there are other ways of dealing with facts than of using what we normally think of as factual writing. It is open to approach them through fiction or to take up the spectator role in other ways in order to meditate on their pattern and form.

The section which follows attempts to document some of these possibilities. The reader may like to carry forward from Part One some of the issues raised there about the processes of de-centring and re-integration and also about development of the writer's resources. Some of the writing included here allows a look at such processes at work. What is the pattern of development in the young writer's effective use of transactional functions?

Equally he may like to think about the converse of the question posed at the end of Part Two. Why is it that an understanding of the transactional function in writing seems of much later development than that of the poetic? Is it enough to say that it is to do with the process of de-centring – of seeing the world as something separate from oneself? What, for example, do we understand by the notion of relevance in writing – relevant to whom, or to what?

There is one issue which poses itself rather sharply in looking at much informative writing in school. How far is it always possible to keep a balance in one's judgement between the adequacy of a writer's resources for the job and the effect of the particular situation which he has had to meet? About factual writing for example Sarah (a thirteen year old) had this to say:

I detest writing for History and often for Geography – I think its absolutley loathsome writing down fact after fact of history when one can easily read it from the book you are copying from. It is dead boring. Geography is not *so* bad, though still pretty bad, as again, boring facts must be written down in as good a way as possible and that is so tedious.

Happily it is not always like this:

I think it is nice to be writing down facts that are new to you and are interesting and also knowing that the essay is right (Mary aged 13).

But one suspects that a lot of informative writing in school may take place in a situation which the writer, rightly or wrongly, interprets merely as calling for a routine performance.

An aspect of this perhaps is that it may not always be clear to the writer whether the situation is one which allows him to use writing to work through ideas for himself in a tentative and exploratory way, coming to discriminate their relevance and power; or whether his situation presupposes that this has already been done and he is in the business of setting down an account for somebody else. The baldness, even the muddle, of young writers early attempts to inform may have something to do with this. Similarly 'irrelevance' may speak not so much of an incapacity to distinguish what is central from what is peripheral, but of the process of making such distinctions at a stage before the writer is able to turn his thinking outwards into a public account.

Finally, the reader may like to reflect on the processes involved in some of the ways of handling information other than the strictly informative account.

The first three pieces all demonstrate one way of dealing with information – by classifying it, while wholly subordinating the personality of the writer. The writers are concerned with the organization of known information into a form that makes a general statement about that area of knowledge; and the form includes the use of specialized terms – fulcrum, intersection, sacrum, and so on.

1 Levers

A lever is basicly a bar used for lifting things, by pressing on one end. The weight being lifted is called the *load* and the pressing is called the *effort*. All levers need a support and this is called the *fulcrum*. Also all levers have *ratios*. There are three different classes of levers and they all have a load, an effort and a fulcrum. The first class lever is like the one below.

[DIAGRAM]

On this lever the load-arm is three feet long and the effort arm is six feet long. The effort arm is twice as long as the load arm, so there is a 2:1 ratio. On every lever all the ratios are the same, so on this lever, if the effort arm is moved down 10" then the load arm will come up 5".

The second-class lever is like a wheelbarrow. On this lever the fulcrum is on the wheel and the load is near the middle.

[DIAGRAM]

The third-class lever is a pulley. On the pulley below there are six strings and the load is 18lbs. Those six strings divide the weight of the load six times and $18 \div 6 = 3$ so the effort will only need to be 3lbs to balance it. If the 3lbs is moved down six inches then the 18lbs or the load will only go up 1 inch because there is 6:1 ratio.

[DIAGRAM]

Pulleys are used in garages to lift car engines because the engine can be lifted up or let down, just a fraction of an inch, at a time. On the pulley I have drawn all the ratios are 6:1 so if it was used in a garage to lift an engine and the effort of 3lbs was pushed down 3 inches the load of 18lbs (which would only be part of an engine) would only come up half-an-inch.

Doors are levers as well. The hinges are the fulcrum, the door is the load and the effort is when you open the door with a handle.

Scissors are levers. The pivot is the fulcrum, the load is the thing you are cutting, and the effort is your fingers pressing in the two holes.

Girl *aged 11*

2

Triangulation is the way in which the map is constructed. The person who is making the survey chooses two points. These can be any fairly short distance apart. Then the person chooses a landmark, e.g. a hill top. He then views this landmark from the first point. Then he works out the direction of the landmark. He then draws a line on his paper in that direction. He then repeats this from the other point and draws another line. At the intersection he puts a cross. This is the tip of his landmark. The person then chooses another landmark and he does exactly the same again. Inside all of his smaller triangles he picks out a lesser landmark e.g. a post office. He positions this on his paper as above and then he continues to do this until he has enough places on the paper. The rest of the map is compiled by measuring from one point to another.

Girl *aged 12*

3

The human skeleton consists of two groups of bones. The *vertebral column*, *spine* and *skull* and the limb girdles (and limbs. The upper limb girdle is called the *Petoral girdle* and the lower is called the *Pelvic girdle*. The Vertebral column is made up of small bones called *cervical vertebrae*. These can be divided into groups. Thus the bones of the neck are the *atlas vertebrae*. Those of the chest are called the *thoracic vertebrae*, those of the small of the back are the *lumbar vertebrae*. Those of the pelvic girdle are fused to form the *sacrum*. The tail of the column is the *vertical vertebrae*.

Boy *aged 13*

Very often we may not detach the 'information' from the context in which we learn it; and this is especially true of younger children. Pieces 4 and 5 are reports which still organize information, but now the writers are also involved with the circumstances in which they encountered the facts.

4 A Visit to Castleton - the Dream Cave

After descending a few steps we arrived at the Dream Cave, where hundreds of stalactites hang, of all shapes and sizes. The longest stalactite is a little less than four feet in length, and nearly meets a stalagmite. Only $1\frac{1}{2}$ inches separate the two. When they meet they will form a pillar, from roof to floor. They will probably meet in a thousand years. As we looked around the guide told us that a lot of the stalagmites and stalctites resemble things. One looked like a stork standing on one leg, another a stuffed partridge hanging up, and another looked rather like an elephant, as well as those there were many others. There were two stalactites which had grown side by side until they measured 9ins in height, then they joined, to give the impression of Siamese twins. Some start growing rather slenderly, then fatten at the top, looking like carrots. But I think the strangest of all, were the helectites, these were the short twisted or hook-shaped growths, shooting out sideways from a wall.

Boy *aged 11*

5

Jill and me got a bowl with a $\frac{1}{2}$ litre of water and put an egg in it and it sunk to the bottom. Then we got another bowl of water and put six spoons of salt in and when we put the egg in it floated. Then we put three spoons of salt in the first bowl but the egg wouldn't float. So the egg only floats in the water with most salt in. I think it must be like the Dead Sea. Mrs Norris gave me and Jill an egg each for our tea.

Girl *aged 11*

In the next four pieces, the writers are handling the information in a new way. Implicit in all of them is the idea that these facts concern *me*: the children are dealing not only with the information itself, but also with their own reactions to it. They are concerned with the information for its own sake, and intrigued by its implications.

6 Rome

pepple in Rome did biled there flors on pilers so that the warm air would not be traped   so they bilt Ther houses on pilers so the warm air could come out so Thay could ceep warm becaues Thay had no roffes. and they didernt have a propper flor thay had mosaices little bits of square mosaices and it was all diffrernt patterns   and The roman had slaves and sumtimes the Roman made there slaves fight there bess men and they rily used to kill them and everybody ust to wash (watch) eaven Little girls and boys   and Roman bilt there own roads and they ust to mesher them by seeing how many stones up to London   and Romans where very clean and The Roman had central heating   and the Roman done there summs diffrent and Thay rote diffrernt here are the Roman numbers
I II III IV V VI VII VIII IX X XI XII XIII

Janet *aged 7*

7 Machines help

Levers lift things. This is an everyday lever, your mother may use it. It is a spoon opening a tin. There are three points need to make a lever. An effort a balance point and a load. A can-opener is another lever. The effort is the hand, the blade is the balance point and the can is the load. A ramp entitles you to go higher or lower. But if you want to go up a ramp you would have to travel a greater distance. A screw is a ramp it is like a spiral staircase. You never get something for nothing. A car consists of many small machines to make a big machine. There is one lever in a car that even mentions the word lever in its name. It is the gear lever.

Boy *aged 10*

8 How the sea began

This is probably another piece of fiction because nobody really knows how the sea began, people just try to imagine and nearly always their imaginations are different. My explanation would be that about three billion years ago. For that is, about as old as the earth and I think that the sea is about as old. The earth was a ball of very hot whirling gases gradually the flaming gases cooled down and began to liquefy and the earth became a molten mass of liquid. The materials in this molten mass sorted themselves out according to their weight, the heaviest in the centre, the lighter ones near the outside and the lightest ones making the outside. The earth is still the same today the centre of the earth is a ball of molten iron, very nearly as hot as it was three billion years ago. Around it is a middle layer, not fully hardened, of a dark rock called basalt. Beyond that is a hard outer shell, very thin and made up of solid basalt and granite.

Boy *aged 11*

9

There are many difficult things in coal mining. Many men get killed. It is very dangerous working in a coal mine. You can get crushed or die because of loss of air. Sometimes men die because of fumes. There are only wooden props and posts that support the roof of a mine; they could easily snap then the roof would cave in.

Once on T.V. there was a young lady married a man. They were happy until the man got a job as a miner. The woman didn't see the man so much so she divorced him.

Girl *aged 11*

Information becomes relevant when we use it, and there are more ways of using it than by writing directly to inform, as we see here. The authors of pieces 10 and 11 are pushing out into other ways of structuring what they know. They are using the information as a starting point for their own purposes, although these are, as yet, fairly unsophisticated. Under the surface fictions, however, there is a hard core of knowledge which is taking on a new vitality for the writer as it is used.

10 A Plague in My Village

In 600 AD there was a plague in my village and the plague was called the black fever and it was very dangerous indeed many people died, and very few survived. I kept away from everyone who had the disease, it was very very very dangerous indeed. The people were very friendly but I did not want to know them. Eighty-nine people had died in just this week. Then we decided it must be god who was doing this to us so we decided we would say a pray about seventine times a day and go to church four times on sunday and to go and worship him in church every day.

Time went by and more and more people had died and only about eight had survived. There was a funeral about four times a day or more, lots of people were crying because there husbands or wives had died because of this disease. Children had died as well and had suffered many pains. It was unhappy for those who had the desease the red black come out worse all oyer and by now there was only a few people left. Yells would come from people at night when the moon was low and the moon was resting on the water which was nearby. Crying would also be going on and waking all those that were still a life awake. It was very very unhappy indeed. And lots of people died over one disease a dangerous desaese called BLACK fever.

Girl *aged 12*

11 Why Athens

Athens. This is the city I'd like. A sort of peaceful city. A city that enjoys life. A city that takes pride in its community – They're loyal. This is a unique city. One of great architecture. Such beautiful cities and buildings. The people had good relations with other towns and countries. They traded with each other.

They're great artists, music lovers. This city has poets, writers, many famous sculptors. Their plays are famous. Joyful to watch. You learn from their plays.

They also have many games. Everybody enjoyed life.

You may say that Athens is a soft city, but I say that the Athenians fight only if they have to and they fight well, and I also say that those who think they are strong and pick on the weak ones, beware, for the weak might be stronger than you the strong think. The strong will be slack and won't be expecting.

Athens the city of peace, enjoyment, loyalty and skill.

ATHENS FOR ME.

Boy *aged 12*

One of the most difficult and demanding jobs is to use the information we possess as a basis for speculation. In piece 12, John is painstakingly and logically erecting a careful structure of speculation and underpinning it all the time with unobtrusively employed knowledge. The ability to ask 'What will happen if . . . ?' and to answer the question oneself, shows a delicate control of both the material and the form.

12 Social Studies

If we look back through history at any one incident if that did not happen or is something else happened instead we could have a totally different way of life. I think that any main dissisions that are taken should be aimed at the future. So it will not affect the future population in any way that would harm their ways of life. Political discissions are very important to the future. If China was allowed to join the UN this could help the future tremedesly. We would not have to worrie as much as we do now about war. America is the only obsital in the way for some reasons the Americans don't want China is the united nations. I think the should be allowed in because they are the third world power and with their strength and scientific knowhow we would not have to worry about any world wars for a good many years to come or until China leaves the United Nations but they haven't joined yet so there is still uncertaintie weather China will start a war or not on one of her neighbouring countries. I think that the more power that is given to the UN the less wars there will be If China was a member of the UN Vietnam war could stop because China is supplying North Vietnam with arms. I think that China will become a member of the UN within the next two years weather America likes it or not. But even if China became a member there is no saying if she will agree on most political oppinions of Russia and America. The Vietnam war has been going for six years now. The American soldiers have forgotten what they are fighting for the war is being dragged on. America still regonise Chang as the China power. Britain regonised the Communist government years ago. There is no sence in not recognising something that exists America is dreaming over this. Mayby they think Mao wont live much longer and mayby then they hope for the country to go back to the nationists government. Mao had an answer to this it was the red gaurds. Mao backed the red guards and gave them the power to do what they want. I think this was Mao's way of showing he was not finished.

John *aged 14*

Pieces 13–15 all show alternative ways of handling information: 13 chats to us, 14 is a piece of rhetoric, 15 is out-and-out invention. But underlying each is a considerable sophistication in the way the knowledge is organized and employed. Despite its disarming chattiness, 13 is asking important questions about our relations with our own bodies, and with Science; 14 is controlling information about Imperial Rome and politics, and using it to persuade us to agree with the writer's own viewpoint – a subtle achievement; and *The Log of the Ark*, quite apart from its control of style, is working out the writer's fascination with a whole range of information, from Biblical studies to Natural History, and placing it all in the context of his basic concern – how Noah and the other humans react to the disaster they are faced with.

13

It makes you feel a bit sick doesn't it at first just talking and thinking about your inside, all modgy and ugh. I mean you look allright from the outside it hard to think that inside you're like that. But that's me inside I wonder what we'd look like without the outside bit? but we couldn't hold together without skin, could we? All those things though, white blood corpuscles and red ones and bacteria, I can't really imagine that they're inside me now, this very minute. I've got a little cut on my finger and there's just a tiny speck of blood there, I can't see how all those many cells and things can be swimming about in that little speck. And those bacteria, they must look horrible, fancy having live things under your skin. Its hard to believe and I can't imagine it at all, they must be so very tiny, white blood cells as well on guard duty ready to get rid of the bacteria, can it really be happening *now* in me? Perhaps while I'm writing this there's a little battle going on somewhere perhpas in that cut on my finger, I wonder if they know what they're doing, or if they think about it. You tend to think of them as charators don't you? with human charactoristics.

Girl *aged 18*

14 Caesar deserved to die

Rejoice! People of Rome & it's great Empire! Caesar is dead. You are free at last from that tyrant, Caesar. The peoples Rome can once more rule their city and land; decide for themselves whether they should send their sons into battle. Never again will there be such a tyrant leading Rome. Never again will one man decide laws.

Caesar was a friend to me & I to him, but I could never agree with his way of thought in law. Oh, yes Caesar did give lamnd to the poor, but what are you to the better when your sons are taken away from it to bloody wars?? What use is land without workers? Any fool could see he was just trying to be popular. And why didn't you see? Caesar was teaching you not to think; not to question his laws; not to think of the Empire as a whole, but to think of your own small piece. In fact to think like him. To think selfishly when a whole Empire is at stake is criminal, Caesar thought selfishly. He was dictator: his word was the last word. He used his power in the wrong way. Why, because Caesar was dictator should he judge legal cases himself? How, could a man make a law completely of his own will without consulting anyone else, let alone the people who it affected? Caesar was like our master and we his slave. He could treat us any way he chose. He could consult us, or he could chose not to. Caesar chose not to. We feel as a slave feels when his master takes away his old tunic and presents him with a new one that doesn't fit & the master refuses to listen to his pleas.

Caesar did too much with his power. He treated it in the way of small child; he did too much with it. He too far. He made himself a God & put his statue in the temples for us to worship. He put his head on our coins.

Why do think we Romans voted for self-government? To save us from a dictator's selfish rule. When a dictator rules it is natural that we should protest. When Caesar took no heed of our pleas, what could we do but get rid of him? It is unfortunate that it had to be death, but it was the only way.

Do not weep, Romans, at a tyrant's death; look forward to a pleasant future.

Boy *aged 12*

15 The Log of the Ark

Twenty-fourth day of life on the 'ark'

Today we were greatly grieved to find that the calf that was born two weeks ago is dead of anthrax.

The smell from the animals' quarters is unbearable and we shall have to clean out all the stalls and cages, though I don't how we shall clear out the fiercer animals stalls. There was a terrible storm earlier this afternoon and we were afraid that at any moment we would be capsized. The animals have not taken to ship life very well and keep us awake at night with their many different noises. Shem's wife looked rather pale today so we kept her in bed and made her as comforable as possible.

Twenty-fifth day

Today we set about cleaning the animals' quarters. We started off with the cow as her dung smells terrible. She was rather wild so we had to lassoo and bind her before we could clean her stall out. We were so intent on our work that we didn't realize it was feeding time until my wife rushed down to us terrified and said that one of the lions had broken loose and was frightening the elephants. After some time we managed to entice the lion back to its stall with some meat. After feeding the animals we had a meal ourselves and prayed to God.

Twenty-sixth day

Today we found that the female cat has three kittens one male and two female. Also the father mouse we found had made a hole in one of the horse's fodder bags and much of the grain has fallen on the floor. We have reason to believe that the woodworm have bred in the main mast. We are greatly in need of fresh water and have decided to put out tubs each night to catch the rain. Also, food for the elephants and other herbiferous creatures is becoming scarce as the rain manages to get at the stores of dried palm leaves and grass, and soak them.

Twenty-seventh day

The rabbits have had babies and we think we shall have to kill them for fresh meat unless the rains abate soon. Ham has made himself a fishing net so that we can get food for ourselves from the sea. We are thinking of feeding the carniverous animals on fish in the near future if nothing crops up. Today we saw a school of whales and managed to kill a young calf which will serve us and the flesh-eating animals food for perhaps more than a week. The water is thick with dead bodies and torn up bushes and trees we managed to salvage one or two bushes for fodder.

Twenty-eighth day

The male cat attacked the mice early this morning and killed three of the young ones. The blackbirds, sparrows and robins all had laid eggs sometime today. Mrs. Hen is a great help, she provides us with breakfast. Mrs. Duck also lays eggs and these are used as food for the stoats and weasels. There are many frog, toad and newt tadpoles swimming around in their basin. We may have to use some of these as food for the water-insects. The male fox killed the cockerel today and nearly the hen as well. Shem's wife is a bit better and we think she suffers from food-poisoning.

Twenty-ninth day
The storm still rages on and the women are frightened that it will never stop even my sons are a little uneasy. The ants are busy and have laid dozens of eggs. When they are hatched I think I shall set the ant-eaters on them as we can not have them all over the place. The female gorrila has had a male child and that is good as we were forced to kill the father because he was diseased. We can not wash our clothes as they would never dry in the rain. Ham and Japheth's wives were engaged in mending one of the sails as it ripped. We hope that, with the will of God better times will come

Girl *aged 12*

The final piece is the beginning of an essay by a sixth-form girl, moving easily into the complex business of historical theory. The question she is asked is simple, and might have been answered in a simple way; but the material available to Hilary is complex, and so is her treatment of it. The control she has over her material, and the logical, cool and disciplined patterns of thought she is holding in balance, show confidence and a sure hand. This is the culmination of one kind of 'handling information': the academic writer who has learned the full importance of 'facts' and who can manage with assurance the subtle and difficult business of selecting and interpreting the relevant ones. She produces her own theories, substantiates them, and has before her a clear image of her own purposes in writing the way she does.

16 'All James I's problems were inherited.' Do you agree?
In 1603 James became King of England, and his reign showed a marked progress in the questioning of royal power and the revolt against authority which was to culminate in civil war. Was this tendency a continuation of an already-established pattern, or a result of James' policy and government?

James was already King of Scotland and one of his first problems was to adapt his theories and methods of government in Scotland to the different situation in England. On the whole, he had ruled Scotland successfully and efficiently, and this, together with a personal conceit, led him to underestimate the difficulties of ruling England. He failed to realise the importance of Parliament; in Scotland it was the nobles who wielded political power, and this led him to make many of his more capable advisers peers, thus weakening his influence in the Commons.

James, although learned, had not the traditional dignity of a monarch – his tastes and behaviour were sometimes vulgar and slovenly, and this diminished popular respect for him. He was made over-confident by the warm reception which he received at his accession, which he took to be a tribute to his personality when in fact it was merely relief at having the succession finally settled. This tended to make him unaware of the full extent of the problems and tensions in the relationship between himself and his people, and particularly his parliaments.

However, it is time to say that he inherited many of these problems from Elizabeth. The last years of her reign had been in many ways a period of decline, with faction at court leading to inefficient government, and growing agitation in Parliament for freedom to discuss all aspects of national affairs, and more freedom from royal control. She had managed to keep these demands at bay by the force of her eloquent speeches and her personality, which aroused admiration and loyalty, but the will of the sovereign was no longer the supreme force in the state, and the nobility and gentry were emerging as a ruling class, represented by Parliament.

James also inherited a difficult economic situation. The size of the debt which Elizabeth left is uncertain, but nevertheless the country was impoverished by years of war with Spain, and money was raised by out-of-date subsidies, collected by an inefficient administrative system. Trade and commercial expansion was restricted by the monopoly system, and the piracy and trade with the Spanish colonies was based on a policy of war with Spain. The price rise had affected the monarchy itself, and the court could no longer afford to be so attractive to the rising nobility. With fewer new personalities, the existing nobility drew together in cliques and factions, making government inefficient and affecting royal prestige.

Hilary *aged 17*

Part Four
Four Pupils and their Writing

This section presents the writing of four school pupils, at various stages of the period of formal education. Michael, at seven, is at the beginning, just learning how to make the pen part of his hand. Kerry, at nine, has already succeeded to some extent in that, although in terms of the same image, she often suffers cramp. Chris, at fourteen, faces the full pressure of the examination system, making as it does impossible demands on his writing repertoire. And lastly Jessica, at eighteen, who has achieved her majority, and knows it.

Ideally, of course, a section on development should contain the total output of perhaps two individuals during the eleven years represented here. That would enable us to follow the writers through the ups and downs of learning to write. We would note, no doubt, that progress is slow, although not necessarily gradual; that a writer does not develop on all fronts at once; that there is some relation between what a person reads and what he writes.

Although we have been unable to assemble such case studies, nevertheless, we feel that the four writers are useful examples. They mark four distinct phases. To begin with, everyone has to start somewhere somehow: Michael's work speaks loudly of what a struggle it is. Next, if a person is ever to see the written language as an active part of language activity, he must derive satisfaction for at least some of the time. That is true of some of Kerry's work, perhaps significantly, in story and poem. Then of course, there is the march towards the fifth year of secondary school, which places such a stress on being able to write in many different ways in order to present appropriate credentials to an examiner. What are one's chances of survival? Thus Chris. And finally, if you survive that, you may spread your wings, and savour your power. Hence Jessica.

Michael

Michael, at just over seven years of age, is in his last term in the Infants' School. The organization in his classroom is flexible enough to allow for a wide range of individual concerns and rates of development, and within its supportive and sympathetic framework he may to a large extent choose to read or write, paint, model or act out the things which seem important or interesting to him.

The ability to 'fix' his thoughts in words on paper is only a recent acquisition, an acquisition in which he feels pride and enjoyment and in which – through his teacher's pleasure – he feels the approbation of the adult world. He writes mainly series of simple, direct statements about particular happenings, and the loftier generalizations of a later stage are yet to come.

1

My dady gos to work   he works at control flamboilers   the best thing my dady likse is tacing me to work   I have a brother   he has to go to the dentist today and I hav a sister whos allways doing things rong   my Mumy is allways leting me do things.

2

On Sataday we did some tiye and dye   When the tiye and dye was dry we cut the string and when we opened it up there was a luvleey patten.

3

George Best spat at the ref and chuced mud at him   and George Best got sent off the feeld   he had to stand on the side of the feeld and wach.

4

This is a picher of Tescos   it cott alite on Friday   there was 20 fire engins and 2 fire tenders   it was alite for 2 hours. All of the people who was in Tescos had to leave all there goodse in the shop   to people was taken to hospital and one firemam.

5

At six o'clock forkt litning started   I went to the window and wached the forkt litning going across the sky.

6

On sunday I went to a carnivill   on the other side of the road I saw John and John saw me   I got a little jelle monster   the monster had a little pese where you lik it and it stiks on a lot of things.

7

Last night we was going to have a fire becos of the grass that we had cut. When he lifded all the grass up a lot of smoke came up so dady dug a hole a big hole   and put all the grass in the hole.

We may see the beginnings of speculation, and an attempt to handle causality.

8

If I was not me I would be an engine ear   geting a lot of Electrisate to make the washing masheens go and All the litse. You make Electricsate by stem terbinse.

9 My Adventure Playground

If I had a Adventure playground I wood put a sand pit for the 2s 3s and 4s and the biger boys and gils and I wood have a climin fram and ground and a ice cream van. But it must not be that drivs away evry night   it had to stay for all day. There wood be a big big tunnl and a slid and swings   but the swings wood be much diffrent swings than the ones in the rec.

10

The Mother ship has lost all its oxeejn (oxygen) and they are breeving as little oxeejn as they can. they think what coolst all the trubl was a meetee-arite hit the front of the Mother ship and all the fuel has run out.

When his class had carried out a project on Australia, Michael was asked to imagine that he was Johnny (an Australian boy) and to write about what his life was like – quite a formidable task. But after an initial stumble in his piece of writing, and after he has collected his sister and brother for imaginative company and comfort, he sustains the idea extremely well.

11 Australia

Johnny lives in Australia. it is one of the bigest country's in the woruld and I have a sister and my brother. I live in the middl of Australia. it takes four weeks to get to the nerist town   in summer we get rain. In winter we go swiming becos we have nice warm days   I dont go to school becos it is to far so I lisen to transister   it is a to way transister. The black men help us to do the work in Australia   my dady is the oner of the cattel station.

The kangaroo is called a joey and we hav kaloa bears to in our conutry. Becos we are so far away we hardly go there.

We have never seen snow for a long time. After our hoilday in Melbourne I come back to where I live in Australia.

Naturally, the information which was available for Michael to use in his picture of Australian life was limited by the books which he could find and the information which the teacher had given to the children. In that case there was not much difficulty for him to see what she wanted to 'get back' from him in his writing. But it was rather different when all the children went to the zoo, because all sorts of important and interesting things happened quite individually to each child:

12 A visit to the zoo

At the zoo it was good becos I have never been befor. At the zoo I saw some camles thay smelt horrble one camle had fur coming of for summer. We went in the moonlite house it was dark inside. The animals in it come out nigt. I liked the rinos best I dident see the hipos.

When we went I went on the coch and I sat next to David and Stephen. We shared our sweets Stephens were nise We dident see the sea loins becos they were to sleepy. The gibbons were funny becos they swung about on the cages showing of. The peacock was showing of as well he was showing his tail to evrybody I had cheas rolls and appl and some sweets and crisps I bouhgt a orange dringk and a chock Ics.

Fortunately the teacher was understanding and she knew that cheese rolls and Stephen's sweets might have been even *more* important to Michael than the sea lions, so she didn't suggest that they were 'irrelevant' or 'unnecessary' – learning about relevance would come slowly quite a lot later on.

The teacher showed the same understanding of the unwitting problems of the young writer when he wrote about which part of the year was busiest for the farmer. Michael started with some quite impersonal generalized comments about the rural scene in spring, but when he comes to winter time and remembers snow and sledges and snowballs, then the memories and associations are so strong and personal that they push the impersonal farmer and his rural annual timetable right out of the picture!

13

In spring evrything is alive and it is sunny evry day and when you go out in your car you see sheep and cows out in the feelds and the farmer is plowing or he is driving his trakter.
but in winter it is dull and the farmer puts his cows and sheep away in a shed some pepl like going on slejes when it snowes. Last winter my sister biult a snow man and at school we frow snow balls at eash uther I thing I like winter best.

Fantasy and imagination are also at work in more direct ways, fed by the stories and poems which have been read to Michael by his teacher and which he can now read for himself. They are, of course, mediated by the pressures and values of the society which surrounds him (the nature of the rewards in the following pieces seem more than familiar!).

14 Magic

I wave my wand and what happens
I wish a tree would fall down
and a lot of gold fall out
into a sack so I will be rich
I wave my wand and what happens
I wish I was on the sea bed.

15 The man who made machinnes
A BOOKLET

Once there was a man coold Mr Maxie. He inventid all sotse of machinnes. He makes plastic bag machinnes and paint machinnes. He yousis a machinne to cut iron   One day when he was making one that made ice crem a hevee peese of iron fell on Mr Maxies arm.

Mr Maxie went to the hospitl   he liked it. Soon he colde come out of hospitl and start work agan   the first machinne he made when he came out of hospitl was a pen machinne. He liked making machinnes a lot.

He siad to himself   at last I have finisht all the machinnes that I wanted to make. Now all I have to do is get the men to make the paint and the plastic bags   So he got the men and soone he had all of the machinnes going. He had to get 12

Mr Maxie did not haf to work eney more becos the men worked for him. The End

16 The four men and the whale
A BOOKLET

Once there was a wale who lived in a cave. One day four men went out on a speed boat   one man said to anuther man   what is that silverish gray thing in the midl of the sea   it looks like a submureen.

One man said   it is to big to be a submureen   what can it be   here is a rope   make a lasooe with the rope   get your diving sootse on becos it is diving under water   I will fro the lasooe on to the tale now.

I will tell you why we have to put the lasooe on that silverish gray thing becos we are runing out of ful. Then the silverish gray thing dived under water   the four men fell out of the boat.

It was all rite when they fell out of the boat   thay swam about under

sea. A man said   we have lost the cheef   were can he be   One man said
Look I have fownd a under water cave.

The uther men came and the three of them went into the under water
cave   and they fownd the cheef in the cave triyeing to pull a box of
tresher out of the cave. One diver popted up then he popted under and
said   I can see anuther speed boat what has got a hook on it. He popted
up agan and got the hook   thay had lost a lot of oxeejane. Soon they had
the tresher in the boat and the four men got into the boat.

But they still had to find out wat the silverish gray thing was. Then thay
saw it and thay fownd out wat it was   it was a wale. The four men went
on to Aisland and they fownd a lot of speers.

So thay went back onto the boat and throw the speers down the walse
throt and thay kild the wale   and the four men went on to land with the
tresher and the men came famas and thay all lived happaly.

Michael does not yet see himself as a 'writer' – one who has made the purposes of
writing his own – he is too young yet. But already the pressures are there which
suggest to him that writing is merely a tool to serve extrinsic school purposes
(passing examinations?). How many of Michael's contemporaries have a writer in
the family other than those involved in the educational field – certainly Michael
hasn't. Perhaps already he has had formulated for him a set of notions of what
education is about which are very different from those underlying the practices of
the teachers who teach him. It would be interesting to speculate what led to
Michael cutting out and bringing to school the newspaper picture for which he
wrote the following caption:

17

This is a man who tried to jump out of a window because he didn't pass his
exam   To policemen stopped him.

Kerry

Kerry, a nine year old, working in a kindly and vigorous classroom, is confronted,
like Michael, with the two kinds of concern discussed in Parts Two and Three.
Like him, too, her ability to write with conviction and satisfaction in all areas of
those concerns is not an even one; she is much stronger when it comes to 'sharing
experience' than when 'handling information'.

Unlike Michael, she does consider herself to be a writer, although as yet that
confidence manifests itself only in her poems and stories.

To establish, then, her strengths. She can write a narrative story with gusto,

gusto actually reinforced by her wayward punctuation. All of her writing presented here comes from a project on ships.

1 The Secret of the Deep Sea Wreck

Dawn breaks with a cool breeze, the sun gleaming strongly down onto a huge handsome house, 'Gwinline', a great clammer rose from the lawn, panting loudly a stubby dog ran exhausted after a group of boys, a great crowd of them. A deafening noise. Oh! what a terrible din. A elderly lady appeared at the door of 'Gwinline' come in boys dinner's ready. Pity I was enjoying myself, a noise rose up above the din, by see you this afternoon! A wiry boy separated from the crowd, curly ginger hair, and a football in his hands. Me better be going to Goodbye. A tiny fellow disappeared through the huge black gates. The lady was still standing. Nice fellows Peter, weren't they. What's the tiny fellow called, oh you fall over him Mum, his names Gwen, and that wiry fellow is Frank. Come on it is dinnertime. Well, have you been wondering what name the dog has got, his name is Shadow. The house is silent but not for long, Frank and, where was Gwen, Frank was bouncing his ball up the long track to the house, beautiful Gwenline. Peter looked out the window, Mum where is Gwen, Frank is there but – Gwen isn't. Golly Frank looked worried. Finish your breakfast cried Peter's mother. I have, by mum, I'm off! Where are you going but Peter had gone. Frank you look worried, Frank what is wrong? Where is Gwen? Before he's dinner, Frank stutted, He went down on the beach, on a boat, I watched him. He disappeared, he is dead! He's dead cried Peter, well i think he is sobbed Frank. Don't waste time with questions! They ran so fast they collasped on the beach exhausted. Can you swim, they both said. Yes! Like a nightmare, I must say! Down down and stil down, lucky they were both good swimmers Where is Gwen? Is he died or is he alive? Where is Gwen? Suddenly Peter who was leading stood motionless at a sight, a great sight. A huge everlasting wreck. Don't stare, we are looking Gwen you know. Oh Golly where is Gwen. Gwen Gwen it was Gwen suddenly cried Frank, lying still in that wreck. It was. Without a word they made their way into the deserted wreck, fear gripped them. A noise made them tensed. Come on or you will get hurt, it was Gwen, Yes it was Gwen. A rough man behind him. Now for heavens sake shush! He put his finger across his mouth for a sign of silence. Go on boy. A rough voice echoed. Keep you here, don't need a guard, nobody ever comes round ere. You won't have a nice time tomorrow, your father will be poor before you know, and if he ain't you shall die, I will hold you as hostage tomorrow, Lad you going to be in trouble tomorrow. Do you hear. He grabbed Gwen by the collar and threw him roughly on the stone floor. I will go now, Leaving him unconscious on the floor he left. Immediately Peter stepped forward, lucky he is unconscious, he hates swimming and we will have to swim. Lucky he's light too, said Frank. Up, up, to the surface. Gwen was safe. Suddenly a police car roared past, he stopped it, trouble down there sergeant. I will deal with them thieves. Thanks kids, have a medal. What an adventure. Gwen is safe!

We can observe here an important realization of the writer of fiction: not only do events proceed in time, and characters act and are acted upon; they also speak out loud, and think inside their heads. We can see, in this piece, welded together, the dialogue of external speech, and the monologue inside Peter's head.

More deliberately constructed are her poems. Here are two from the project, representing her most advanced attempts to *make* things in words.

2 The Shipwreck

The impatient waves
lashing against the
straining boat, the sky
looking heavy with rain.
Feet skuttling anxious by on deck.
Terrified, disaster has befallen us, torrents
Of rains falls, heavily.
The waves now pounding roughly against the swaying boat.
Were done for, finished.
Given up hope of every living!
All hopes have gone.
Brave minute boats, help is coming,
Through all the dangers of the sea, help is coming,
We're safe, safe!
Out of danger now.
Help is on its way.
A miracle has come.
Safe, safe from the dangers of the sea
Safe!

3 The Elegant Mermaid

The elegant mermaid sitting on her throne, her locks of hair swaying
    behind her,
Her tail coiled behind her.
Her voice ringing like bells,
Sweet and charming.

But her eyes filled with evil.
Death to all men who dare to enter her kingdom.
The waves iridescent, rocking gently.
Creatures jumping to attention at her orders.
It's her kingdom!
All hers!
Every rock, every wave, is hers!
Every man is hers!

Her achievement in these three pieces must be related to many factors, two of which deserve special mention. Of central importance is the fact that what is to count as appropriate is *hers* to decide; the reader, or probably in her case the teacher, can agree or disagree with the 'arrangements', but can have no substantial voice in any alterations. Hardly less central is her experience of relevant kinds of language. She has already at nine internalized many of the structures other writers have used in the writing of stories and poems. If, as we suggested in the introduction, the central aspect of writing is to keep one's eye on the object, and let the language flow, Kerry has a wide range of language to flow.

If we contrast the story and poems with her writings to 'handle information', the picture is a very different one. She tackles a simple report (not that reporting is simple, but that in relation to all the ways children are asked to handle information, reporting is the simplest), and manages to do something of the job, even to the extent of writing as though she were genuinely informing a reader who didn't already know.

4 Ships

Victory, a very famous ship, is the fifth ship of the Royal Navy to bear this name. The first Victory, launched in 1559, of 800 tons was the flagship of Sir John Hawkins at the defeat of the Spanish Armada in 1588. In 1778 France entered the war on the side of the American colonists and Victory was hurried to Portsmouth and in May she hoisted the flag of Admiral Keppel in command of the Channel Fleet. And Nelson soon left England, later Victory led his people into battle, but Victory was damaged, so very damaged she had to be towed to Gibraltar to be repaired and soon with a crew aboard she sailed for Portsmouth and soon she had battered sides and creaking masts. On December 22nd she arrived at Sheerness and here she had the proudest flag she was ever priveleged to wear. Well now I will tell you about the inside of Victory. This is the quarter deck.

[ILLUSTRATION]

This report is possible for her because she can marshal the relevant facts along a time continuum. The narrative principle, if you like, becomes the central principle of organization. When, however, a principle of organization other than narrative is required, Kerry flounders about. She either throws the facts together in almost any order, or, when she can, shifts as quickly as possible back into a time sequence.

5

A powerboat is made from fibreglass, its heavyier at the back than the front. The shape of the ship enables it to move. It skiddes across the water. Once they had a Powerboat race. They started at Portsmouth. The sampan is like a floating market, it is a flat boat and it is moved by a pole. The pole is stuck in the ground under the water and above the water the boat moves. It is like a floating market with about five boats (sampans) moving along the water with food stored in the boat. It is a lovely sight! Aircraft carrier is a ship that carrys aircraft. It is made from steel. It has a jetty leaning out from the side. A river Barge is transport for Africa. The bottom of the River Barge is wood. The other parts are steel. It takes people across rivers. It is a good transport. It is build like a raft. It carrys oil. A passenger Liner carrys passengers. It is made of steel. It is a very tall ship. A racing Yacht has a huge sail. Well two huge sails. It billows out in the wind. The racing Yacht is made of fibreglass or wood.

6 Pirates and piracy

Pirates are called Buccaneers for they once where on land and were killing wild animals and were buccaning meat so they called Buccaneers. That is how they got their names, and they were throw from the land so they went to sea, Pirates. They fought cruelly with the Spaniards. Sir Henry Morgan was a pirate, he was a Welshman. One account tells us he was kidnapped as a boy and sole as a slave in the West Indies. He escaped from his owner and joined the crew of a pirate ship. Privateers were paid by the government to be a pirate and he couldn't be hanged if he was caught. Pirates skuttled ships, (sank them). They have codes, they must not break them. Pirates have very strong ships, (very fast.)

In these pieces, the process of writing has become little more than exercises in the random retrieval of information. The difficulty lies not so much in the ability to remember discrete and relevant facts, but in finding an appropriate frame in terms of which these facts can be shown to be related. Whereas with her story and poems she had the double advantage of choosing her own ground, and using language with which she is deeply familiar, here she has the double disadvantage of having to meet other people's criteria of relevance in language which is still not hers to command.

Finally, a piece which begins in one camp and ends in another. Here she has given up 'handling information' in mid-stream – has turned aside from those tasks which do not bring satisfaction – and has moved into 'sharing experience'. There, certainly, she does know what she is up to.

7 Old Father Thames

Queen Elizabeth's palace was at Greenwich, she was often to be seen in her royal barge as she travelled from whitehall. Charles II was a keen sailor, he soon started a fashion, by having a yacht for racing, a pretty thing, says Pepys.

Gilded barges were for the King and Queen, they carried the Queen and King. Merchant ships carryed cargo. Light skiffs carrys one passenger. Wherries are used for taking passengers across and round the river, a rowing boat. Slow barges were loaded with coal and grain. Racing hoys are speedy little ships, Charles II liked racing and so they had these racing hoys. Queen Elizabeth I and Charles II were often seen by the river. The river was like a road because they liked the river. They had to go by river for Whitehall was on the river and they went there a lot. More nearer the sea the larger ships were seen, sovereign of the sea, great barges and so on. A ship would be used as a taxi. The buildings towering up, our small little wherry straining, pushing her way to safety. The engine rumbling away, the waves lapping gently against my boat, the boat floating swiftly across the water, night is here, lights vanishing, one by one.

The lamps gleaming, like cats eyes on the peaceful water. All is silent, Everything is motionless.

Silent follows.

Chris

Chris is not a boy who is obviously destined for an academic two- or three-year course in the sixth form. Perhaps he will take an A-level or two; perhaps he will stay on into the sixth year to retake some O-levels if he doesn't pass them first time. At present he is in his fourth year at secondary school, though some of the work looked at here dates from his third.

He is beginning the fairly long run-in to O-level (or CSE, if he isn't 'good' enough for GCE). His environment, partly in consequence, differs from Michael's or Kerry's in a number of ways. His timetable is differentiated rather than 'free-flowing'. That is to say he studies separate 'subjects', moving across the day from classroom to classroom, from empire to empire, and writes for separate subject teachers. He has to cope too in his writing with much stronger expectations from outside. He must write in this way for History, in that for Geography. His Physics teacher will want one thing, his English teacher another – and so on. In addition he will have to set himself increasingly towards mastering a set of specific performances – the GCE note, the three/four side essay (neither too long nor too short). What will count in the end will be not only his interest and his knowledge but whether he can market it.

So his general development is realized in a fairly specific context. First though, to chart the general. Like Kerry he is happier when he is 'sharing experience' than 'handling information'. (The concentration of the curriculum, of course, is most strong at the point where he is weakest.) Like Kerry too he finds it difficult to exchange a narrative principle of organization for a classificatory. His difficulty is most marked in his writing of History. Here is part of Essay 6, followed by part of Essay 7 one third of the way through his third year.

1 Essay 6

Dudley was completly different person from seymour, he was a protestant. He wanted the protestant religion to be the only religion. So in 1552 he brought out a protestant prayer book and all R.C. bishops were imprisoned including Gardener, bishop of Winchester and Bonner bishop of London. Now he wanted to get rid of the Catholics, but before he could do this he heard from Edward's doctors that Edward was going to die soon of T.B. Dudley then dropped all other plans and started thinking about the next heir to the thrown. The three possibilitys were all female. One was Mary Tudor, Elizabeth Tudor and Mary queen of Scotland. He wanted to marry one of these so that when they became queen he would be king. The problem was which one to marry. Mary Tudor was R.C. he could not marry he Elizabeth Tudor was whatever the king was and Mary queen of Scots was R.C. So he looks for the next person down the line and finds her but first he has to convince Edward VI that Lady Jane Grey really should be the queen. His reasons for getting rid of the other three heirs was that Mary Tudor but her father might not have been Henry VIII and therefore she would not be able to rule. Elizabeths mother was exicuted for adulter and the daughter might do the same.

2 Essay 7

Just then a famous painter called Holbien had painted Anne of Cleves and in the picture she looked very beutiful. So Anne was to come to England to get married. When Henry sees her he calls her a FAT FLANDERS COW because she was fat, ugly and stupid but Henry has to get married and in the church he starts looking for a better looking lady.

He finds a better looking lady in Catherine Howard. Henry divorced Anne of Cleves and sent her back to Germany with enough money to last her whole life. Catherine Howarg was the neice of the Duke Norfolk who was the most powerful baron and since he was Roman Catholic he could get all the barons together and take England. Cromwell tried to warn Henry, and he thanked him for his advice and had him executed for treason. Then Henry marryied Howard. England wanted a deffence and this is where the English navy was formed. Before Henry designed the ships they were big, thick and heavy. When Henry designed his ships they were thin and had three rows of cannons instead of one. Now the chance of England being attacked died away because Spain and France had started fighting. Then Henry decided he wanted to do some invading of his own. Since England was not then a part of England Henry wanted them to join. Henry also thought it would be easy because all of the good soldiers had been killed by Walsey's army. Henry's army was beaten at the battle and they had retreated to a position in Sollway Moss which was at the end of a valley. There was little hills at each side were Henry's army took the cannons off the ships and put them on the hills. When the Scots saw Henry's army at the end of the valley all helpless and weak they started a charge. When they got to where the cannons were the cannons fired and with grapeshots as amunition they whiped out all the scotish army (8–700 men) and only 7 Englishmen were killed. When the Scotish king hears the news he dies of a heart attack and he leaves his one week old daughter to be a queen. When Henry died he left 90 ships and made the Royal navy strongest in the world.

We may note here too the absence of any defined sense of the reader – an important matter for the writer who seeks to inform. Much of either piece seems to take the form of a stream of annotations for himself rather than an attempt to engage with a reader separate from himself for whom he must modify his utterance accordingly. (This – as much perhaps as his dependence on narrative – lies behind the tendency to shift out of the past into the present tense.)

Frankly though, as important as Chris's development seems the process by which in the long run it is achieved. Not only must Chris learn to cope with the demands of the subject, but also with the expectations of particular teachers. Here are sections of the actual manuscript. They illustrate the process more vividly than I can describe.

3

> DON'T MAKE UP HISTORY!!(

Rubbed

posibilitys were all female, one ~~and~~
Mary Tudar , Elizabeth Tudar and
Mary queen of Scot~~land~~. He ~~wanted
to marry one of these~~ so that when
they ~~became~~ queen he would be king
The problem was ~~which~~ one to marry
Mary Tudar ~~was~~ R.C. he could not
marry her, Elizabeth Tudar ~~was~~ ~~a~~
~~catholic~~ Was whatever the king was
and Mary queen of Scots was R.C.
So he looks for the next person down the
line (and sends) but first he ~~has~~ to convince
Edward VI that Lady Jane Greg really
shoud be the queen. His reasons for geting rid of the other ~~three~~ heirs ~~was~~ ~~was~~
that Mary Tudar but her father might
not have been Henry VIII and therefore
she would not be able to rule. Elizabeths
mother was executed for adultery and
the daughter might do the same
Mary queen of Scots was married to
Francis of France and they were enemy

4 HISTORY ESSAYS ARE WRITTEN IN
THE <u>PAST - TENSE</u>!!!

of the good soldiers had been killed by
Walsey's army. Henry's army was beaten at
the battle and they had retreated to
a position in Solloway Moss which was
at the end of a valley. There was little hills
at each side where Henry's army took
the cannons off the ships and put them
on the hills. When the Scots saw Henry's
army at the end of the valley all helpless and weak they started a charge
When they got to were the cannons
were the cannons fired ant with
grape shots as own ammunition they
whiped out all the scotish army (2-700
men) and only ⑦ English men were
killed when the scotish king hears
the news he dies of a heart attack
and he leaves his one week old daughter to be queen. When Henry died
he left 90 ships and Made the Royal
navy the stongyest in the world
CATHERNE PARR? DEVAUATION?
continues with scotland?

Chris wrote seventeen essays in 'History' for this teacher in his third year. These are the marks, and the comments:

1. 7/20. Details and persons need to be included.
2. 10/20. Spelling atrocious.
3. 12/20. Watch your tenses but getting better.
4. 4/20. Go through this work and put it into the PAST TENSE.
5. Unmarked.
6. 4/20. Do your spelling corrections. Very poor work.
7. 8/20. Catherine Parr? Devaluation? Continues war with Scotland?
8. Unmarked.
9. Unmarked, except for a tick at the end.
10. 9/20. Poor correlation of facts.
11. 5/20. TENSES! Unfinished poor work.
12. Unmarked, except for a tick.
13. 9/20. SPELLING ! ! DO YOUR CORRECTIONS !
14. 14/20.
15. 13/20.
16. 13/20.
17. 14/20.

The only positive encouragement in words was 'getting better' at the end of essay three. Elsewhere, there is a tick for a fact simply recorded. The work reproduced above shows how meticulously mistakes in spelling and tense were pointed out (though not corrected). Perhaps he was encouraged orally in class to apply his own deductive powers to understanding and interpreting the facts as he saw them, but his uninspired efforts to do so in writing are heavily penalized – DON'T MAKE UP HISTORY! ! ! It takes all year, but by the end of his third year and the beginning of his fourth he seems finally to have 'learned' his lesson. In essay seventeen the trick is earning the tick at the rate of one for one.

5   Colonisation

James, like every other king was wanted
to expand his land. There were several
ways you couldddhis, conquer, explore
or settle James started & settling. He
started sending English settlers to Ulster.
He gained three things by sending people
to Ulster. One was that he could
withdraw the English army from
Ireland, two he got rid of the unym-
ployed and three he got rid of Hugh
O'Neil. This was a success so he sent
people to the Americas. The first
successful attempt was in Virginia
in 1607 The first stat was called
Jamestown after James. ~~Jamestown~~.
Tablacco grew in Virginia and the
Virginia Co of London was for founded.
The second successful attempt was by
the pilgrim fathers at Plymouth 1620
America Another attempt which was
successful, was successful by mistake.
Settlers took off for Virginia but

Narrative has been exchanged for number: the classificatory principle is secure. In real terms though, has he learned to do more than receive the facts and give them back again undistorted by the intervention of his own imagination, speculative or deductive powers?

By contrast, his Geography work (there is roughly the same amount as History) hasn't a single mark by the teacher on it. We have Chris's second- and third-year folders, and the only sign of it being read by a teacher is the simple word 'Finish' in red at the bottom of one of the cyclostyled maps.

The work in his third year folder covered (at the rate of two or three pages each) Chicago, the North Lands, the Growth of Russia, Time, Hong Kong, Manchuria, India, Siberia. Chris has learnt how to marshal his facts, and present them in a clear, simple, well-organized, interesting way. The style, though basically similar to that of the History essays, is more relaxed and confident, and the facts flow well. This seems to suggest greater interest and involvement, although the piece is impersonal, objective:

6 Siberia

In Siberia winters are very cold with temperatures as low as minus 70 degrees C. The tempriture falls as low as this because the air is very clear and the ground can radiate heat out into space. This makes the ground and the air above it, cold. As the air cools it contracts and becomes denser and it lies heavily on the ground. It does not move easily because it is so dense. It is called POLAR CONTINENTAL AIR because it originates in the Polar Regions of a large continent. Sometimes this air spreads out across Europe bringing a spell of cold clear weather. This cold weather and the cooling of the ground causes the water in the soil to freeze. This freezing goes down to great depths even 1,000 feet. The summers are not long enough for this to thaw out and so it remains perminantly frozen. This is called PERMAFROST. The soil above the Permafrost is very marshy in summer because the soil water cannot drain away as the frozen subsoil is impervious.

Is there something of the wonder still in 'even 1,000 feet'?

By contrast, it seems a pity that the boy's creative imagination in a subject with such obvious potential as Religious Education should apparently only find an outlet in the drawing of a little boat (HMS Noah's Ark) on a map of the relevant part of the world ('B— quite a good map – but I don't like your boat. Please add more place names.'), or the interpolation of an incongruity such as 'Bothe emphasise a part played by women in the nude' in piece 7.

7 The Acts of The Apostles

The Acts of the Apostals is a link between the story of Jesus Christ and the growth of the Christian church. It is a book containing storys of plots and persicution and imprisonment, of escapes of storms and shipwrecks of riots and controversy. It relates how the church began and how it spread from Jerusalem through Palestine to antioch and Asia Minors, to Europe and then to the capital of the Roman Empire, all within 30 years 30AD to 60AD. This Book is the only written brigde between the person of Jesus and the religion of Christianity. It tells use how the church was created. *The Litarary Background of the Act of the Apostles.*

It is generally agread that St Lukes gospal and the Acts have the same author, the reasons for this are,

1. The new religion of Christ is seen as a universal religion. It is for all men regardless of their race or nationality. 2. Both books emphasise the power of the Holy Spirit. 3. Both books show that there authors cared very greatly for the poor. 4. Bothe emphasise a part played by women in the nude. 5. Perhaps the most important reason is that both books are adressed to the same person Theophilus.

If the same person wrote the Gospal of Luke and the Acts he is the most important writer in the Bible. He has written $\frac{1}{4}$ of the new testement by himself. Without him many of the storys about Jesus would be unknown and we would have no knolegde of the begginings of the Christian church.

We wonder if Chris ever wrote in Religious Education about the fact that he had once discussed Religion with Archbishop Makarios.

There is a variety of writing in his English folder: stories and poems, a play, letters, discussions, arguments. Not all of this writing is concerned with 'sharing experience'. But in this area Chris seemed more involved and more secure. The following piece, with its contrast to the RE work preceding, suggests the greater confidence Chris has when his writing can make contact with his own experience, and when he can draw on his resources of speech.

8 A Conflict Between my parents idea of religion, and mine

My parents are church mad. (all Greeks are). They only go on Sunday but for a total of 4 hours. At Christmas and easter we go 6 hours a day for 1 week, you would think they would have a break but they just continue. If you leave the church you shall miss some of it and that is very bad. You can't even chew or read. I think this is all wrong. You should be able to chew at least, and I just can't see whats wrong with reading because I cant even understand what there saying most of the time.

Once not long ago my father was ill, my mum went to the church with fifty pounds worth of Jewelry and gave it to the preist as a gift to God so that my father could be well again. I was against this and I told them so and they told me it always works. Then I told them that when English people are ill they dont offer money and they still get better, to this they didn't answer. I also used to go to greek class at a church and I used to be the best pupil and they were always after me to be a priest (HUH), and I always used to be in plays and once I talked about religion to the President of Cyprus who is an archibishop and he agreed with me in about two cases. My parents want me to be connected with the church but because of my ideas about it its impossible.

Last Christmas I sat next to a girl and my mother made me move because we were in church, I am against this as well, what could happen just by sitting next to a girl.

The Greek church has been in issolation for about 100 years now, things havent changed for a hundred years

I would like to reproduce a piece Chris wrote in Biology in his *first* year, because it is a statement of attitude which I think was sincerely felt at the time, even if the analogy was suggested by the teacher.

9

We do not know everything about animals. You can find something about a cat that a scientist does not know. Most of the animals have escaped mans eyes and we do not know much about them. Some animals fly to warmer countrys which makes it difficult to find out about it. You have to be a sort of detective to find out about animals. You have to look for a lot of things. A real detective has to use his eyes and his hand to find out how the crime was done. He has to make a full record of the things he has found out of the crime. An idea of something like this in Biology is called Hypothesis. This word means something has to be tested. If the idea is no good the have a different idea in its place

It's a good analogy. Yet we often hear it said that a subject only becomes interesting in the sixth form (sometimes even not until University) because, it is supposed, there is 'so much spadework to be done first'? But here is another analogy. The most enthusiastic and careful spadeworkers are those who feel the excitement of possible discovery, who have a sense that they are playing an important part in discovering clues or amassing evidence in support of a hypothesis; not those who are given a spade and told where to dig, and have no concept of the value of what they might 'find', or much idea of its importance to them. Especially when they know that what they will 'find' will have been planted there for them in the first place.

Three years after the hopefulness of his first year's work in Biology (and we have read it all), we find most of his work in the subject to be diagrams and notes which list an extremely complex series of 'names' for 'things'. This 'Spirogyra' example is typical.

10 Spirogyra
Spirogyra is a simple green plant

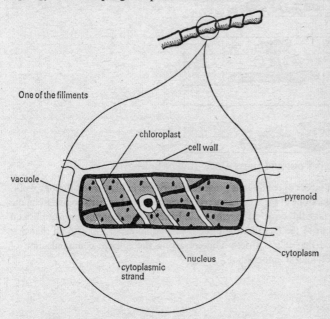

Growth Cells divide transversely, increase in length.
Reproduction Sexual and Asexual.
                 Asexual = fragmentation, brakes into pieces and continues
                 to grow.
Sexual Conjugation (diagrams).

Sexual Reproduction in Spirogyra

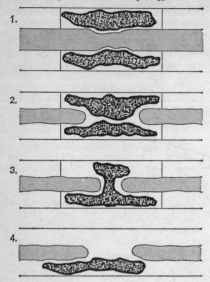

This comes out and starts a new row of Spirogyra

Two short pieces of continuous prose have survived in his written Biology work. We reproduce one of them in manuscript because of the teacher's comment on the piece. We take this criticism to refer *not* to handwriting, margins, paragraphs and the like; but to the fact that the piece *is* in continuous prose, with all that that entails, and that this is strictly unnecessary in the efficient communication of relevant 'biological' information.

11   Breathing in Fish

Fish are vertebrate animals living in fresh or sea water. They are also Poikilothermic which is an animal whos body tempriture varies with that of its surroundings. The scales of a fish are bony plates made in the skin. the scales overlap each other and give a protective covering. The age of the fish can be estimated by the ammount of rings on the scales.

Oxygen dissolved in the water is absorbed by the gills. The movement of the mouth and operculum are co-ordinated to produce a stream of water, in through the mouth, over the gills and out through the operculum. There are usually four gills on each side. These gills are many bony fragments with smaller fragments on them.

Although there is more oxygen in air than in water a fish will suffocate in water. This is because the muscular system of the mouth and the operculum which can work in water will not work in air.

        Breathing in Amphibians.

You must tidy up your work and present it in a more orderly fashion   (B⁻) 8-10-71

The pattern is followed in Physics. If there is any commitment to the matter in hand, any excitement at being on the brink of discovery, it is well hidden. He carries out the correct procedures and having obtained the correct results records them accurately with complete calm:

12

The flask shown was connected to a vacuume pump, the clip was opened and the air pumped out. The clip was closed, the rubber tube disconected from the pump and the flask was weighed. The clip was now opened and the flask was weighed with air. The increase in weight gave the weight of air in the flask. The volume of the air was found by filling the flask with water and pouring this water into a measuring cylinder clearly the volume of the air which was in the flask is the same as the volume of this water.

Chris may indeed be one of the minority who can survive until the sixth form. He has shown his resilience throughout the third-year struggle with History, and in almost all his writing for the different 'subjects' shown increasing confidence in following the formula to which his work must increasingly tend.

But is it the 'right' formula? The right formula for what? Surely there are many other, more attractive possibilities, which are still not being fully explored?

Jessica

Jessica is seventeen, a member of the specialist sixth form of a girls' grammar school. Unlike Michael or Kerry she is no longer still relatively a learner; nor like Chris is she forcing herself unwillingly for much of the time into someone else's pattern. She is more able with words than many who are her elders. Her expectations fit pretty well with those of the school. The pace of her learning is relatively unforced.

Thus the strengths which she is seeking in her writing are of an order which we have only so far glimpsed and which remain outside the experience of many children during their time at school. Broadly speaking the long struggle with the classificatory principle of organization is over. Unlike Chris there is no limit to her capacity to thread her way through fact. She is freed now to explore the power of abstraction itself. It is not to exaggerate the potential excitement of the road which lies before her to say that she can set out now to explain and control the world.

In her writing of History for example, one of the three subjects in which she specializes (the others are Physics and English), the focus of her attention lies in the sweep of her general argument. To put it epigrammatically, event exists to substantiate generalization, rather than generalization to organize event.

1 'Elizabeth learned her main lesson in statecraft before she came to the throne.'

While Elizabeth was still in the womb of Anne Boleyn, her existence became a matter of momentus importance. It decided the lonely fate of Catherine of Aragon, urged Henry to tear the English church out of the clutches of the Pope, aroused the hopes of the protestants and cast fear into the hearts of all orthodox catholics. Few children can have had so many hopes pinned on them. As Lucy Baldwin Smith writes in 'The Elizabethan Epic': 'From the moment of her conception, the princess's sex and legitimacy were crucial factors in the course of European History.'

And what style too: we are in the hands of a professional, of an expert writing to experts.

Her birth, in the form of a girl, was a terrible let down, Henry was devastated, the Protestants appalled, it seemed the English church had been rent assunder to assure the legitimacy of a mere girl. Such feelings must surely have offended the infant Elizabeth whose mother was as disappointed in her sex as was, Henry. Nor was Elizabeth's childhood secure and peaceful. Within few years of her birth she was to watch Jane Seymour win the heart of her father and feel her own position lapped by uncertainty. The ways of the court held no magical mysteries for Elizabeth but instead hard realities which she was herself deeply embroiled in. She felt her shaky position rocked by a succession of mothers and witnessed executions and guiles. Unlike most adolescents her flirtings ended not in scoldings but in death and violence. Seymour her artfull step-father and would-be husband was smashed under her nose and Elizabeth was forced to play cool to keep her life. She thus learnt early to show no hint of her emotions.

How much has it mattered behind the poised historical allusiveness of all this that she too is a girl?

During Edward's reign, she watched her brother being used by his councillors, during Mary's she felt again the thinness of the thread on which her life hung. She was imprisoened and plotted against before she even reached the throne and she survived execution only through the compassion of her sister.

And here is the pivotal transition:

Thus when Elizabeth succeeded Mary to the throne of England in 1558 she was certainly not unprepared for the rigours of kingship.

It is now the statecraft which is to be documented.

She displayed her knowledge of statecraft throughout her reign. She had seen marriage after marriage of her fathers fall into disaster and she knew the loss of power that getting married would entail, thus she was unwilling to embroil herself in one, yet she knew how best to use her suitors. She never insulted any of them by rejecting them but kept them dangling for her hand, in a position where they could do her no harm. By rejecting marriage she neither earned the displeasure of her people by marrying abroad, thus allowing foreign influence into Britain, nor did she enrage their petty strifes by raising an English man to the level of King.

She was equally wise in her religious settlement, she had no desires to conform the kingdom to a set train of thought, and rarely did she put any-one to death for religious reasons. She realsied that diversity of thought was not harmful when it was unspoken and not stirred up, and thus she followed a moderate policy, compromising between the protestant and catholic religions, She would have no Pope but nor did she claim to be herself the supreme head of the church, only its 'supreme governor'!

In all, her reign began a period of relative peace, during which the country slowly recovered from the rigours of Edward and Mary's reign. She centralised her government, choosing good men to serve her whom she picked from the poorer gentry whose loyalty she could thus depend on as their estate rested solely in her hands. However probably the greatest asset to the success of her reign was that she lived long enough to ensure that her policies grew to be accepted.

Jessica then has developed an understanding which is important for the writer of history: that the power of abstraction lies not only in its capacity to organize particulars, but in the possibility of using that organization to develop a coherent and related argument. Essentially, the process on which this understanding depends would seem to be the ability to develop an interrelated hierarchy of generalizations on top of the basic level of particulars. Specifically, the relationships are as follows:

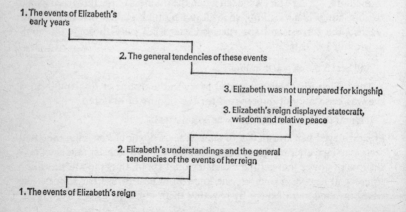

In terms of the diagram the structure of Jessica's argument turns on her powers of abstraction at the intermediate level 2. This level she has to operate in two directions. It is the link between the particular events (the facts of history both before and after Elizabeth's accession) and the interpretative statements of the highest level of generality. The particular and the general, in other words, are connected by this level. But this level is also the point where the substance of the argument has to be developed. These intermediate generalizations have also to be balanced and assessed against each other. For the argument is that there is a connection between Elizabeth's early experience and her subsequent statecraft as Queen. The connection accordingly has to be established between the tendencies in the events before her accession and the tendencies of her later actions. (She had seen marriage after marriage of her father fall into disaster and she knew the loss of power that getting married would entail.) All this is a quite different order of abstraction from any we have seen so far.

Here then is a new possibility which Jessica is exploring, and in fact on it will rest substantially her effectiveness as a thinker. For argument is given power, not by its most general statements (nor by its particulars), but by the intermediate statements on which those more general statements rest. That Elizabeth's reign displayed statecraft, wisdom and relative peace tells us little; but that the implications of statecraft are balance between opposing factions, that Elizabeth's refusal to marry reconciled at one stroke the chauvinistic and the ambitious and that the implications of Henry's succession of marriages were to make Elizabeth aware of marriage's importance as a political tactic – this lends to the general an explanatory power which is worth having.

Since, though, it is fundamentally a new sort of endeavour for Jessica it is also the one which gives her most difficulty. How far in Jessica's historical piece is this level really examined? (How far too is this connected with the confident tone of historian to historian which she has set herself to take up and which is at first sight one of the strengths of the piece?) In her writing in Physics, for example, classification gives her no problems. Here is a question on a worksheet:

2 Questions (Nuffield Physics)
1. S^1 and S^2 are two sources of sound of the same frequency. An observer at A hardly hears any sound. How would you account for this? Sketch the path he would have to follow in order to keep the sound he hears at a minimum as he moves towards the sources.

She is aware of the principle that two sound waves interrupt each other where the crest of one coincides with the trough of the other: classifying this particular instance is something she takes in her stride.

The observer at A hears very little sound because the waves from S^1 and S^2 are causing destructive interference at A. ie the crests of one wave are filling up the troughs of another so that the waves are cancelled out.

Much of the message is carried in the diagram.

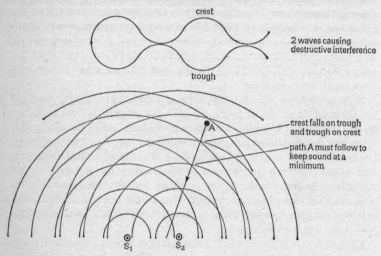

Here, though, is a later question.

In an interference experiment with waves cancellation occurs at points where a peak coincides with a trough. Does this violate the principle of the conservation of energy? Discuss.

The answer (we believe) is roughly this: that the law of conservation of energy (that in any isolated system the total amount of energy remains unchanged) is not violated because in this instance the energy is re-distributed, extra energy appearing where the waves reinforce each other. Cancellation in other words implies no change in the total amount of energy present in the environment of this experiment.

To arrive at this answer one must bring together the implications of two high-level principles and to generate a speculative solution as to how their apparent contradiction can be reconciled. Since the task faces her with that middle order of abstraction which she is still relatively inexperienced in exploring systematically, it is not surprising that she has difficulty in orienting herself.

3

2 separate waves which are identical, for example 2 sound waves with the same wavelength and frequency will set up vibrations in the air which our ears will interpret as sound when the vibrations hit our eardrums. The waves have energy and do work in setting up vibrations and when the vibrations cease the energy will be in the form of heat. Yet these same two waves if sent out so that they cancel each other out will cause no vibrations, where has the energy gone?

It seems to me . . .

It is her own hypothesis: compare the tone of her historical writing.

. . . this is similar to 2 balls of the same mass and velocity, banging into a third ball at the same moment, so that the third ball remains stationary and once again the energy apparently vanishes. In the case of the balls, the third ball is probably slightly compressed and the kinetic energy converted into potential energy as the third ball can now re-expand. Maybe something similar occurs when two waves come together and cancell each other out. It could be that the atoms which carry the vibrations when they meet up with equal and opposite vibrations become compressed.

But at this point a principle occurs which would conflict with this explanation.

But on second thoughts this is unlikely, for if the vibrations are equal and opposite they will have enough energy to stop each other and no more. The only other thing I can think of is that as the vibrations stop each other the energy is given off in the form of heat. If this is so the principle of conservation of energy is not violated.

It is a nice piece of speculation. (Perhaps the arrival is less important than the travel.) Her difficulty perhaps lies centrally with the fact that the range of possible hypotheses is a relatively open one: experience counts here quite as much as language. To operate with certainty she would need to operate systematically rather than by intuitive leaps. But the real point is that she cannot operate other than intuitively – she must make what she can of what she knows – and language here permits her to do it. It is an example of the sort of writing one needs to represent possibilities to oneself at a stage of exploration rather than of confidence (and, by implication, of the sort of reader one needs too).

An interesting aspect of this is that for her the process of formulating the problem in her own terms (it is someone else's problem) is at least as important as the generation of possible solutions. So she has to write her way into the problem in order to select the relevant point of entry into it. On her answer sheet there are actually three separate attempts to do this. If we compare the other two we can see her gradual progress towards a formulation of the question which makes clear to herself its implications.

4

2 separate waves of say sound, cause vibrations which produce the sound, and thus do work in making the vibrations.

If these waves are sent out together in such a way that they cause destructive interference and cancell each other out, no sound is heard, but

2 seperate waves for example sound waves, set up vibrations which we interprate as sound when they hit our ear drums causing them to vibrate. The waves therefore are using energy to move our ear drums which becomes heat energy due to friction.

If the same two waves are sent out in such a way that they cancell each other out, the net result is no vibrations, where has the energy gone?

In another of her pieces of work in Physics though she sets her own problems. This is a record of a piece of scientific investigation initiated and conducted by herself over a period of a fortnight. It is part of the Nuffield programme. The writing is some thirty sides long – itself a feature worth noticing in the context of development. It is a fascinating record of scientific exploration. Having begun by looking at the effects of different sorts of stress on two plasticine pillars, she passes to the more complex problem of investigating the effects of stress on polythene, particularly in relation to colour. We join her as she gathers herself up to deliver her general theory, gliding confidently through the various levels of abstraction. It is an impressive spectacle.

5

To me the fact that the colours in the sequence kept returning in the same order suggested that as the polythene was stretched it was going through a regular pattern, and I thought this might be due to the atoms in their long chains (for polythene being a polymer is made up of long chains of atoms) slipping over each other.

For example, supposing the polythene appeared yellow whenever the atoms in it lay in place in their chains, red as they started to get pulled up over each other, and blue or green as they were falling into their new positions and yellow again as the reached their new positions.

If this were so the colour sequence would continue, getting slower and slower as more and more force was needed to pull the atoms over each other, until the atoms could slide hardly any further without breaking apart. Then if the force was still continued the rows of atoms would start

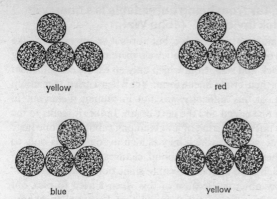

yellow   red

blue   yellow

slipping over each other, and some rows would get over the brink while others would not manage to, those rows which had passed over the brink would look green while those which had not would remain looking red which would explain the red lines that remain in the polythene when it turned green just before it broke.

If further force was applied as the atoms could slip no further they would break apart at some weak point.

Jessica then has achieved her maturity as a writer. This is not to say that she always finds writing easy, nor that she never loses control of the system. For whom would that be true? But she can use the written language now, in a sustained way, at its most powerful levels. She can meet quite particular demands made on her writing from outside and modify her utterance accordingly – witness her writing in History. She can use writing to maintain an exploration of complex sets of ideas over a long period of time – witness her Physics investigation. Her writing in English – the last of her specialisms – merely confirms this. And raises one other point. There is no artistic writing here of course: that has received its curious benediction at O-level. She is launched now in the written word of the academic specialisms. But by contrast with Chris whose problem in his context one might take quite seriously to lie in finding a way of saying anything which was his, one of the many things which it is open to Jessica to explore is what sort of writer she will be. From this perspective her writing in History and in English represent one sort of her scale: the one seeking (and finding) an urbane, public voice, the other relying on a simpler and more direct affirmation of the interest of the material out between writer and reader.

6 'Paradise Lost, far from being unreadable is a quarry in which one can pick up jewels' (John Wain)

Paradise Lost is certainly not unreadable, but nor is it, in my opinion, like a quarry. For this word implies that the jewels therein lie hidden among a jumble of waste, rock and slag, from which only an expert can sift them or recognise them in their crude uncut form. Yet when I tried to pick up jewels in Paradise Lost, my difficulty was not in finding them, but in distinguishing where one ended and the next began. In fact it seems to me that Paradise Lost is not a scattering of jewels among rubble, but one huge jewel with many faces, some of which may hidden in some lights only to leap into life in others. For as one's mood changes different parts of Paradise Lost are heightened by it and seem to shine out above the others, where before they lay obscure. Because of this when I tried to pick out bits of Paradise Lost to write about, I found that I wanted to choose different parts each time I read it, but as I had to make a selection, for I could not copy out the whole poem, I chose the following passages.

The trust in the reader in that is nice. But the writing which at times can merely meander if it wishes, can also tighten to passages of much greater density. Let us leave her halfway through the piece as she classifies the effects of the lines in one of her passages, yet tries to catch too, in the quality of her own writing, something of their power.

This feeling of impenetrable gloom is reinforced in the following lines with both physical and mental images. For neither light nor hope can dwell in Hell, but only darkness and despair. As these images build up the tone slips back into one of dragging horror, as though everything which seeks to break through the gloom of Hell is stifled and smothered, leaving everything within its bounds heavy with gloom. Milton slows the pace by writing in long weary adjectives which both in their shape and meaning radiate despair:

Regions of sorrow, doleful shades, where peace
And rest can never dwell, hope never comes
That comes to all, but torture without end ...

The physical picture of flaming darkness is reinforced by the mental picture of sorrow and hopelessness and a terrible feeling of infinite evil and endlessness is radiated by the tone and pace, the word 'never' is used twice and the menace of 'torture without end' presses on the reader.

Part Five
Difficulties

Probably everybody at some time or another finds difficulty in writing. Only last week my wife was attempting to write a letter to an old family friend whose husband had recently died. 'What can I put?' . . . 'No, that won't do' . . . 'What is there to say?' . . . 'I know what I want to say, but I don't know how on earth to say it.' It took her over two hours to write that letter, consisting of only one side of small notepaper. 'That was the most difficult letter I've ever written.'

She had to take account of the feelings of her reader, a difference in age, to translate her own feelings into words that meant something and weren't mere cliché or pretension and to take account of the permanence of the writing. It may be that that letter would be thrown away after it had been read once, or it could have been shown to friends and perhaps kept and re-read over a long period. So she wanted to write something mainly for now, but also something that would not be too upsetting to her reader at some future reading.

Luckily we don't meet that sort of difficulty very often.

But enough of my wife's difficulties, what about the difficulties she didn't have? As a child she would have overcome the difficulties of handling a pen, of recognizing and forming letters and words, of spelling, of sentence construction, of grammar; and throughout this period become gradually more proficient at changing thought into languuage. She would have learned how to adapt her written language to different situations, how to write in different ways and for different people. She would have met the peculiar difficulties of writing in school: writing to order, writing about things she didn't want to write about, writing for people that would be less interested in *what* she wrote than *how* she wrote it, writing to a time limit or in a specified amount of paper. Probably also she was made to write as a punishment.

And having overcome to a greater or lesser extent all of these problems, writing still presents difficulties!

In this section we attempt to show children working their way through those earlier problems presented by writing; we can see pupils of very different ages and abilities involved in the struggle imposed upon them by the nature of the tasks they have taken on.

When the child begins to write, he is faced with a complex set of difficulties. He has spent the first years of his life mastering the spoken language, and has discovered that speech is a *social* activity – he speaks *to* someone, who usually answers; also that the language comes out as a continuous stream of noise; and that he has at his disposal several different ways of making his meaning clear – intonation, gesture, facial expression, stressing a word, varying the pace and volume and so on – apart from the sounds themselves. Now he has to learn to control an entirely new medium in which there is a whole range of conventions that do not apply to speech. He has to learn the code – to sort out and distinguish letters, and relate them to the noises he makes when he talks; and to start at the left and move to the right in horizontal lines. He has to learn that letters are separated from each other by spaces, and that 'words' are distinguished by having a space before and after them. (Most infants write in one consecutive string of letters, without any indications of word-boundaries, because that is what happens, as close as they can make it, in speech.) He has to learn that, although in speech it's taken for granted that people speak differently from each other, making the sounds in their own individual fashion, in writing there are conventionally approved forms that are demanded.

1

AN EXTRACT FROM A THREE HUNDRED WORD STORY

and it Mighar thans a gan yana yan yana tha gantha gan thaninan hansa gana yan inarg nangan than Sa gan hanan aan than Micana gan yan sa hansa yangan yan Wanine san Inens a n than sa yaina wan ani san inan tha gananthangnan Micnan Sane sann than sa thin yan

Girl *aged 4*

2 My happiest moment

and The Thee I wos. goos dos Inow get e sis we good D. Party I news siwed The wale masfed it a big dog. and away. Les dud wot.

Girl *aged 5*

The impersonality of the writing process – a demand made from outside rather than from within, as with speech – is carried still further; for he discovers that in writing, there is no intonation, no way in which gesture or facial expression or those other helpful features of speech can be transmitted (though children in fact often experiment to find ways in which they *can* use writing for these purposes). Moreover, there is no second person who can immediately encourage with his own responses. Writing is a solitary activity, and only the writer has total control over the product; and the absence of an interlocutor means that everything has to be made explicit and immediately understandable. The writing has to establish its own context, because the reader will not necessarily share the same assumptions and knowledge as the writer.

Finally, the child has to learn that the way in which words are fitted together in writing – its grammar – is different from the corresponding patterns of speech. Speech has hesitations, repetitions, false beginnings, 'ums' and 'ers' and other fillers, quite apart from intonation, stress, pitch and so on; and all of these help us to express ourselves as clearly and directly as possible. Writing has none of these; so its grammar is far more stable and predictable, in order to make the writing intelligible in the absence of its writer.

This is a formidable task; and it should not surprise us, as parents or teachers, when a child fails to move easily from a mastery of speech to a mastery of writing. He may, for example, be not yet physically capable of controlling the writing implement; or he may, indeed, not have mastered speech, or reading, properly, both of which must come before the child can move on confidently to writing. Nor is this all: these difficulties are simply those of controlling the medium, and we have said nothing yet about the many other complex problems the child faces in learning to write fluently – his meeting of demands, both internal and external, his awareness of audience, and his understanding of the purposes for which he is writing.

Much speaking is thinking aloud – allowing what we think to flow out and come up against our companions. Writing, being so much slower, can never quite reach the fluency or spontaneity of speech – how often, after writing, say, a letter to the family, have all of us remembered something we intended to say, but which went out of our minds during the physical job of getting it down on paper?

The permanence of writing pushes us into a much stronger attempt to 'get it right' before we part with it.

3

I did a pattern of the sun and there is a little sun right in the middle of it and a big sun round it.

Girl *aged 6½*

4

The leaf is green and the uthr sid is green but it is not the sam green   The back is lit green and the frunt is doc green and the frunt has veins on and the back has parterrs on and the edges are little.

Boy *aged 7½*

5

My mummy's name is Joy and she has blond curly short hair. And she has green eyes. And my mummy works at the college on a corridor of her own. My mummy's birthday is on the 30th of October. And she watches the moment of truth. And my mummy makes lovely cakes. And other things. My mummy does not wear glasses and she used to type before she was married when she was a teenager, she delivered papers. She does not go to work on Saturdays and Sundays but sometimes she does go to work on Saturdays and Sundays. And she comes home from work at 2 o'clock. Her corridor is B. And there is no one helping her on the corridor but I don't think she minds. Cause sometimes Mrs Lee comes on her corridor my mummy takes something to drink and something to eat to work with her.

My mummy gets things ready for my party. And sometimes I wash and dry the pots for her. My mummy does not smoke.

Girl *aged 8*

If I want to write to tell somebody something that he might not take very well I have to avoid putting anything into words which might be misunderstood; if I were talking to him I could watch his face and probably detect any misunderstanding and put it right immediately. In writing the misunderstanding will last until I have a reply to my letter and I have replied to that. It might of course continue through a whole series of letters to and fro, and never be resolved until we meet and talk about it. Often in speech we rely on facial expression and the mood of the moment to create the right environment for saying what we want to say; how many people I wonder would have the courage to propose marriage by post – or to ask for the loan of a fiver!

So when we ask a child to write we are asking him to cope with a large number of interconnected problems at once; problems deriving from the very nature of the written language. He is expected to be able to encode, to deal with the speed difference between thought and writing and to deal with the absence of the personal relationship whilst the job is going on.

The teacher's job is to help establish the skill and the confidence that enables the child to tackle all these problems at once; it may well be for instance that help with spelling cannot do much for the child without help in other directions. It seems likely, therefore, that the most effective help will be during the actual writing process – dealing with problems as they arise and really concentrating on the idea of language *in operation*.

We should now consider how our audience affects the way we speak or write. When we are speaking we can be sure people are listening – if they are not we perhaps tap them on the shoulder, talk more loudly, grip them by the arm (shout at them?) or else we shut up. When we are writing we don't really *know* that anyone is going to read what we write. The paper may be lost or thrown in the dustbin; there is no real written equivalent of 'Excuse me' or 'Hey Jack', meaning 'I am about to say something, get ready to listen'. If the 'Hey Jack' is accompanied by a belly-laugh, we are signalling to Jack that he is likely to hear a funny story. How do we translate that sort of signal onto paper? How do we get the reader interested enough to read what we write, and at the same time give him some idea of the sort of thing he is going to read about. In the case of a book it may be the picture of a glamorous girl on the front; in a newspaper the head-line, but the child has no such aids – 'Miss, I can't think of a title'. The designer of the book cover thinks he knows the audience who will buy the book, and he caters for that expected audience; the political speaker wants to know what audience to expect before he decides on the tone of his speech or the clothes he will wear. We all probably speak much more freely to someone we can see and judge than to someone on the other end of a telephone, whom we can only judge 'by ear', and certainly we speak more freely with people we know or people who are like the people we know, because we can forecast their reactions to certain things, and adjust what we say accordingly. Indeed with people we know very well we just say something and expect them to understand. A conversation between a man and his wife may proceed almost completely by implication; perhaps they know one another so well that extended speech is not necessary. Let us take what seems at first sight a simple statement like 'It is late, dear'. This could mean 'Why didn't you come in earlier, instead of stopping off at the pub', or 'It's time you got up out of that armchair and made the bedtime drinks', or 'I'm too tired tonight', or 'I'm not too tired tonight'. The relationship between speaker and hearer allows a great deal more to pass than the mere words, and the hearer recognizes which of the many possibilities the speaker had in mind. On the other hand strangers may be completely foxed by 'You must come round and have coffee some time'. Does it mean 'Come whenever you like and there'll be coffee for you', or 'at some date in the future I'll issue a specific invitation to you to come at a certain time – and you'll not be welcome if you turn up unannounced at any other time'?

Writing, even more than speech, demands a knowledge of the likely reactions of the hearer. It is much easier for the child to write for Mrs Brown, whom he knows, rather than for Mrs Smith whom he doesn't. It is not just that he knows the type of subject matter Mrs Brown will praise, but also the type of presentation. It may be that one teacher particularly likes him to put pieces of conversation in his stories; another will take more notice of 'properly formed sentences' with subject and verb than he will of the content of his writing. It is remarkable how quickly children pick up the idiosyncracies of their teachers and modify their writing accordingly. A great deal of school writing is in this way modified by the child's expectation of his teacher's reaction; he has a picture of his reader as a judge – someone who will say 'this is good' and 'that is bad'. It seems unlikely that the child will learn to cope with the 'audience of no immediate response' if the later response nearly always comes from an audience acting in a particular way – being judge or examiner. It is interesting to examine the spoken and written remarks made by a teacher after she has read the child's piece of writing. The remarks may range from 'Watch your spelling 4/10', to 'How did Balius manage to get away from the Red Planet?' We are not suggesting here that spelling is unimportant – merely that a comment like the second is more likely to make the child want to go on writing, with the consequent improvement in spelling and the other parts of his writing that do come with extra practice. There is certainly no evidence to show that 'Learn these 20 spellings' produces better spellers than 'Write another story', or 'Read another book'.

So with all these inter-connected problems facing the child, it is going to be extremely difficult for us to look at a piece of writing and say 'This child's difficulty lies there – and not somewhere else as well.' There can be many different interpretations placed upon any piece of writing; no single interpretation could hope to show everything. So we ask our readers to consider our interpretations as only a part of a very full picture. An interpreter can only wear as many pairs of differently tinted spectacles as are available to him; what we are trying to do here is to suggest some brands of spectacles which others may like to try on. Each of the following pieces has been chosen, not to demonstrate a particular problem, but because together they demonstrate much of the whole field. They cover a wide range of ability, because we need to remember that as one difficulty lessens a whole series of new difficulties takes its place.

This first piece was written in a Physics lesson by a boy of thirteen of above average ability.

6

WRITTEN INSTRUCTIONS A man standing between two parallel cliffs fires a rifle. He hears an echo after $1\frac{1}{2}$ seconds, one after $2\frac{1}{2}$ seconds and one after 4 seconds. Explain how these echoes reach him.

The man fires the rifle, the sound wave takes $\frac{3}{4}$ second to hit cliff 'A' and is reflected to the man taking another $\frac{3}{4}$ second. Thus it takes $1\frac{1}{2}$ seconds to reach the man. The sound wave carries on taking 2 seconds from A till it hits cliff B and is once more reflected to the man. Four seconds later the sound wave has travelled from B to A and to the man.

Boy *aged 13*

We can see from his diagram that he has understood the problem and that he knows the 'answer'. If he did not he would not have been able to put in the

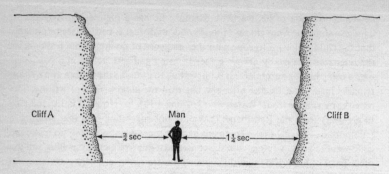

figures $\frac{3}{4}$ second and $1\frac{1}{4}$ seconds. If he had followed up the diagram by drawing three more diagrams – one for each sound wave – he would have demonstrated his understanding and explained the echo phenomenon perfectly adequately. However, writing has caused him some confusion; his third and fourth sentences do not say what he meant them to say. So, whilst he can do the job by diagram and almost certainly in speech 'it goes from here to here to here and back to here in four seconds', he cannot do the same thing in writing. The task of writing seems to have interfered with his understanding of the physical problem. This may be a case in which writing is not the appropriate mode for learning. We can ask ourselves 'What did this boy gain by writing as opposed to doing the job in another way?'

The next three pieces were all written by one boy, aged eleven, the first in a Social Science lesson, the second in a French lesson and the third in an English lesson. He is a member of a group described by their teacher as being of 'generally restricted language ability'.

7

BACKGROUND The pupils were reminded of the work they had done on archaeology and anthropology over the months and told to note, particularly, contrasts in ways of living, especially the contrast provided by modern urban living in an advanced, complex society.

I then wrote brief instructions on the board: 'Imagine that you visit a primitive tribe. Describe your impressions of them and their life and, also, tell us of their reactions to you and the modern gadgets you have with you, e.g. tape-recorder, cine camera, etc.'

I have Just arived in my cunoe at the south american indians country and I banked my cunoe in some bushes and Started to walk. threw. the country where I thought that an indian was gowing to pop out of the bush and so one did. any way to begin with and then there were hundreds they had bow and arrows and they said you white man me no like come. see chefe he says you slave and we went to there camp and saw the chefe and he say waite do you want and we explained to him about the best we could and he said me no understand you we ceap prisoner and we lock prisoners.

Boy *aged 11*

8 Paris

SPOKEN INSTRUCTIONS Write about Britanny, the Basque country, Provence or Paris. Based on information gathered from films, two teachers and (rarely) personal experience.

In Paris it is very posh and there are big buildings. and very big round-about and the cars are different from the English cars there are rest ronts and a English man and lady went into one and they had a very big dinner and when they had finished they went to a sort of Pub it was allso Very posh and they had visitors and violin Players. and they went to lots of other Places to and they had Pictures taken nerly Every where they went they was rely injuing themself the houses are difrent they have nice big Hoteles and nice country to.

Boy *aged 11*

9 Christmas When I was Poor

BACKGROUND The 'lead' lesson included a talk about deprived children, refugees etc., a mime performed by some ten children, and a story about some children who made their own Christmas fun. The pupils were told to imagine themselves as orphans or refugees and to describe their feelings as Christmas approached. A visitor from the Pestalozzi Homes also spoke to the children before they wrote.

My maits and I lost our mothers and fathers it was very sad when it hapened but we are trying to forget about the hole thing and so the days went pasted and Christmas was drawing near and we had now money to get presents. We had an old shake to live in wich we made before but we had nothing to eat no cloths to ceap us warm. the snow was falling now and I sad what shall we do I dont no said John nither do I said bill. I no if we all sit down and think some one mite come up with a sagestyn and so all ten of them sat down and began to think, it was geting dark and John and Jack ho are the two youngest fell asleep and sudenly Ronald came up with a sagestyn. I no lets go carol singing do odd jobs and we shode get some money and so they all stid up except the two youngest which went with

Saramy the eldest and they arranged to meet beck here in about 3 hours and so they did and where they got back they counted their money and they had eleven ponds doing the Jobes as well and they hid the money away in a Safe plase and went to sleep. the money was under Sammys pilor and in the morning they bothe went out the two heldest and bot food and cloths and cars for the litt ones and they had a party after all they had cakes sandwiches and fruits and that was the best christmas party they had ever had and they so hapy after that and they made up a game to get money by doing Jobes and they were called bob and Jobe boys.

Boy *aged 11*

Given that this boy has great difficulty with spelling, sentence construction etc. we have to ask ourselves whether the particular problems inherent in these tasks are reasonable problems to ask him to face.

In the piece 7 ('I have Just arived') he is presented with a task of information retrieval, a task of relating his information to his own experience of urban life, a task of imagination and the complex task of relating all these in the form of a story. With this sort of load we might say that he has come out of it reasonably well. He has concentrated almost completely on the job of producing a story – a mode of writing in which he seems quite confident. Probably the most difficult task for him would be relating the primitive and the urban – he has significantly made no attempt to do this in his writing. It would be interesting to know whether an instruction which merely said 'Write a story about a visit to a primitive tribe' would have produced any different outcome. Similarly we can speculate about what he would have written if his task had been to write about the differences between living in London and living beside the Amazon. As it is we can imagine him sitting there and thinking to himself 'What is it that the teacher wants?'

In piece 8 ('Paris') he seems rather more willing to consider how the information fits into his own world, to the extent of making occasional generalizations: 'The houses are difrent.' He is still to some extent telling a story ('a English man and a lady went into one . . .') but the task of connecting his own life with that of urban Paris is much simpler than is the case of the Amazon. It is interesting that here the idea of comparison is not part of the teacher's instructions. Paris probably appears sufficiently 'real' to have something to do with him, whereas the Amazon could well be closer to the world of fantasy and Martians. It could be important to note that the writing on Paris followed a film – a more direct experience for him – something in which he is happier to become involved.

In piece 9 ('Christmas when I was poor') he again is asked to imagine himself in someone else's shoes. But here he seems to have made quite an effective job of imagining; he is much nearer his home ground and he was given plenty of varied opportunity to get himself 'into' his subject. In the last piece we saw a suggestion of how film had helped in the process; in this one he is even less rushed – a talk, a mime, a story, a visitor – all these would help him to make the experience his own. He has not gone all the way; 'lost our mothers and fathers it was very sad' does not suggest personal involvement – but how does a child picture that happening when it has never really happened to him? But by the time he gets to hiding the money under the pillow that seems much more real, much more of the writer is emerging and the story becomes more interesting as a result.

It is perhaps unfortunate, looking at his three pieces together, that he was given most help in relating to the subject closest to home and least to the most distant.

We can compare those pieces with those on the Amazon and Provence written by another boy in the same group.

10

One day we went sailing and a storm brouded up and the wind changed direction and we hit land I got out of my boat and my friend came with me while walking through the hot jungles of south america we found ourselves in a lot of trouble because standing before us was an indian brave. And pointed at the indian village my friend said what does he want us to do I said that he wanted us to go to his village so we set of hopeing for luck then I thought of somthing that would please the chef I had a cine camra and I asked if I could see the chef they let me and I showed him the camra and he was fasnated untill he tried to shoot it but it dosen't work said the chef in their languich after I used up all the film on the chef and then put it on the projector he was fasnated and began to shot 'oo oo' then he pointed down to the dinner I said that looks dulish after we had finished my friend Joe said 'What was that it looked dulish' and the chef oowoo said 'it was the insides of a snake and frogs eyes. My friend was discusted.

then we went to the river to fish and insted of useing a fishing rod they used a Bow and arrow with a piece of string tied on to the arrow.

Next we went for a hunt but insted of useing a gun they used a spear or a bow and arrow.

Boy *aged 11*

11 Provence

In provence there is bull fighting And on the Rhone there is the bridge of Avignon but it dose not strech out right across the river because part of it was washed-away.

Toulon is on the river.

Benezet built the first bridge of stone across the Rhone. it is called the bridge of Avignon and also on the Rhone is a game played and you use a long pole, a shild, and About twelve men rowing the boat.

Boy *aged 11*

This boy is much more willing to take up the comparison task in his writing on South America, and he shows himself to be quite capable as a story teller. We can see the way in which story telling and the reproduction of information have intertwined; he appears to have a much clearer picture of 'What it is that teacher wants'. He has decided that teacher wants more facts – so when the story begins to flag he has just added some facts on the end. Whilst he was involved in his story the 'facts' took second place, as did questions of spelling and punctuation. He had a story to tell – so he got on and told it, to the extent of generating his own spellings ('languich' – by comparison with the 'idge' or 'itch' sound in 'sandwich'?) In 'Provence' we can see again the boy trying to read his teacher's unspoken intention. At first sight 'Write about Provence' appears an open task ('write whatever you like about Provence') but the writer appears to have interpreted the instruction as 'Put down as many facts as you can for teacher to mark'. The return to the Bridge of Avignon suggests a particular interest; but if that interest did exist it was subsumed to 'fact listing' – 'Toulon is on the river'. Even when describing the game he was content to recount bare facts – somewhat surprising in a boy of eleven who might be expected to go on to tell what happens.

His two pieces show a definite belief that stories are appropriate in one context and not in another. Such awareness of what is acceptable shows how strongly the factor of audience can influence a person's writing.

Another way in which the audience factor makes itself felt is in the question of trust. We are willing to put ourselves into the writing for some people and not for others. In the next piece it could be that the writer was willing to write about what she *does* but not willing to write about what she *is*. Here again the teacher's purposes and those of the pupil do not match. The pupil may have consciously avoided the part of the instruction 'Write about yourself', or alternatively understood something entirely different from what the teacher intended. Here the difficulty is not in the writing; the writer has done a perfectly sound job according to the task she set herself.

12 Preparations for a Picnic

WRITTEN INSTRUCTIONS Write about yourself, about any part of your experience of life so far. You choose what to write about – the list below will suggest ideas. You don't have to stick to the topics listed.

If you are packing up food for a picnic you have to decide what is and what is not needed in the way of food. You should think of food to take which does not take up a lot of room and not take cakes which are made of cream or anything in that line that would squash. For the meal instead of having food that squashes, Cornish Pasties, sandwiches and sausage rolls would be ideal for the occasion as they would not easily squash. When taking the cakes it is best to have plain ordinary buns or any kind of biscuits as these fancy cakes whipped with cream would squash and would not be at all pleasant to eat. When taking the drink it's dangerous to put pop into ordinary glass bottles as they easily brake and could be very dangerous in doing so.

For packing put the food like Cornish Pasties and so forth into plastic containers or wrap them in greaseproof paper. It is also wise to pack the biscuits and the plain buns in the same manner as the Cornish Pasties. For the drink put it in a vacuum flask if it is tea or coffee and if it is pop you could use a vacuum flask or one of those long tupperware beakers would be very handy.

When packing the food into the basket it must not take up a lot of room as there are other things to put in also. The tablecloth must be neatly folded up and that way it will not take up much room in the basket. Packing the right amount of cups, plates and saucers it would be best if they were made out of plastic so they would not easily brake when dropped or banged against one another.

When you arrive at your picnic spot it is best to choose a shady spot and where it is quiet and do not leave any litter where you have picniked. Good picniking.

Girl *aged 13*

We must now look more closely at the questions of organizing material and deciding what is relevant. Before the writer can do these things he has to understand both the material and the task, i.e. to recognize what the subject is about and what he is expected to do with it. He has to make information his own, to see how one bit connects with another and to build up a whole structure of interconnections – an act of building which helps him both to understand for himself and to explain to others.

13 Rotation of Crops

BACKGROUND This was written after I had discussed with them the history behind crop rotation. I then asked them to write it in their own words. No other help was given.

Cavemen first started crop rotation, when they found out that they could not keep growing crops in the same place, so they moved on to another cave and grew crops there, they stayed in one place for about 2 or 3 years.

Then the Roman's came and started another crop rotation they divided the land into 3 parts, one grew corn another grass and the other was left fallow. This was a waste, one third of the land was unproducted. In the Middle-ages there was not many faces, hedges and trees, so there was many crops. In the early 1800s Viscount Townsend who lived in Norfolk went abroad a lot of times, one day he came back from abroad with turnips and clover.

Boy *aged 12*

This boy has been given a number of, to him, disconnected facts. He seems to have recognized that there is a connection, but the connection is not his – it is the textbook's or the teacher's. In attempting to collect them together he has got his facts mixed up historically, and the links between his statements are not made explicit. He has not seen the need to make any general statements about *why* the rotation of crops was necessary.

Similar problems occur in this piece:

14 The importance of Soil to the Farmer and Gardener
BACKGROUND A title to cover various topics done in recent lessons.

Soil is very important to the farmers and gardeners because, of the flowers and vegetables mainly the vegetables. They rely on the vegetables because with out vegetables in some countries they would starve and die. That is in China and India. In America and England the soil is good because of the weather. The soil in our gardens is different from clay because no plants can survive in clay because they haven't enough water and food. The soil has to be good so the farmer can go through it with the plough. The soil has to be so good in the garden because of the gardener digging it. There are many different kinds of soil. In the desert it would be very hard to grow plants at all. there is only one or two plants which can grow in the desert they are cactus and some stuff like straw, which blows about in the wind.

Girl *aged 11*

This girl seems more able than the last writer to perceive connections – but again we see an organizational problem of relating facts to a general framework. As in so much of children's writing in schools (especially secondary schools) the apparent need to regurgitate facts cuts out the necessary thinking about the implications of those facts.

The suggestion here is that the organization of material demands some recognition of a theme or series of themes; we have tried to make a case earlier for children to be given the time to recognize, but surely we must add to that the possibility of the child being allowed to choose his own theme and not being forced to take up the connecting thread which the teacher or the textbook lays down. Progress in thinking lies centrally in making our own connections; if we can take up someone else's connection, accept it and make it our own – that is fine – but if that connection is unacceptable or unrecognized then we must take on the task of forging our own links, of relating what is out there to what we have inside us.

The next three examples all come from Geography lessons. It is probable however that, whilst the main problem they illustrate occurs more often in Geography because of the nature of the subject and way in which it is often taught, these pieces have more general implications for the relationship between the specific and the general right across the curriculum.

15

SPOKEN INSTRUCTIONS Write about the occupations in South West England and where possible give reasons why such occupations exist.

One of the main things farmed on Trenedros farm is dairying. The farmer has thirty cows producing milk. The milk is first sent to a milk station near the farm, from there most of it is sent to London by rail in special glass-lined tanks. In summer sometimes there is a surplus of milk and cheese, butter and dried milk are made, and sometimes Cornish cream.

Another main thing on Trenedros is spring flowers. It is much warmer in Cornwall than most parts of England so they get the advantage of the flowers opening earlier. The picking begins in January when the first buds begin to burst. The people try to pick as many as they can while they are still in bud but usually flowering overtakes them. The journey to London is a long one but it is done as quickly as possible.

Trenedros also grows sugar beet which is sent to a factory in Kidder-minster in the Midlands. It grows kale and dredge corn for cattle food. On the high lands is grass for sheep.

Girl *aged 11*

TEACHER'S COMMENT If you are describing Trenedros you should say it is a typical SW England farm. Tourism!

16

BACKGROUND Essay based on film seen in lesson.

south hill farm have 150 cattle. The west of England were South Hill Farm is, is the wetest part of England. The weathe is milk and wet, which makes good grazing land for cattle. The farmer employs 11 men 1 boy. The cows are milking at 5.3 in the morning and at 8.30 in the afternoon. On another farm there are 15 cows and the milking is done by hand. There are only 2 people on the farm. They don't employ any workers. The churns are left out and a lorry comes and collects the churns and puts empty ones back. All the churns are taken to Brookbridge factory, the poles over the road supply the electricity for the factory the employees come from 7 miles or more. The milk is brought by steam lorry. The churns are heated by steam and the milk is poured away and it curdles it is then put in a cheese press and then it is stalked to ripen off then it is sent off

Boy *aged 11*

17 The countryside around school

BACKGROUND The children were asked to write a short essay on the country-side around the school. No further instructions were given.

The countryside around school is very nice. There is a farm about twenty yards away and the main crops are potatoes and barley. On the front of the school we have five Chesnut trees and a big garden with a tennis court at the bottom, next to the front garden is a main road and the busses go past every half hour, lots of the big lorries pass by every day. Next to the road there is a railway track and the trains go past every half hour. In the back garden there are two greenhouses and one tin shed, we have quite a lot of apple trees and one plum tree and a big vegetable plot.

There is a little beck that flows at the bottom of the back garden and at the side of the front garden. Our school is in the shape of the letter L. Our playing field it is about five acres and we have a cricket pitch and three rugby pitches and three hockey pitches and two tennis courts. We have a net ball pitch and we also play in the Net ball pitch. When you go out of the playground and walk down the back garden path there are two trees planted two yards between each other and now they are fully grown they have made an arch way. If you look out of our form window you can see Skiddaw. The front garden has a drive from the bottom to the front of the School.

Beside the Chesnut trees there is a new art room which has just been built. It is near Wigton and in Cumberland.

Boy *aged 11*

All these writers concentrate on the specific – in the case of 'Trenedros Farm' (piece 15) to the exclusion of the general almost completely. The teacher's comment at the foot consists of a suggestion of how to move into the general and also mentions one occupation which has been missed as a direct result of the way in which the girl tackled the job. Unless spare rooms at Trenedros Farm are let to visitors in the summer there is no way in which she could get tourism in, without altering her whole mode of attack. Similarly she has ruled out any possibility of mentioning fishing, china clay, the naval base at Devonport or the prison on Dartmoor!

Overall she has been asked to do something she could not or would not do: to step back from a view of what happens on one farm to a view of the whole of South West England. It is a problem of stance in relation to her material; we need to consider very seriously the question of how writing can help in the shifting of stance, and of how the writing ties in with other forms of presentation – such as the map, which is in itself, a form of generalization – in so much as it shows a pattern, the way things are related to one another.

In 'South hill farm' (piece 16) we see the same problem, but aggravated by the problems of selection – selection of what is important and what should go where in the writing. Certainly the second and third sentences give general background to what he has to say; but from the writing it is well-nigh impossible to visualize what has happened in the writer's mind between his seeing the film and his writing about it. Also there is little evidence that the film helped to organize the material for him.

In piece 17 ('Countryside around school') we see a list, efficiently done and something to build on. As this boy becomes more of a 'geographer' he will probably develop what he has written into something more general about terrain, vegetation etc. Also he may read 'countryside around' as referring to a rather larger area than he has described. He was not asked directly to generalize, and he has taken the opportunity to collect information for later use. Having recorded, for example, that buses come every half hour, he has the opportunity to recognize the implications of that fact. He needs the specific, as did the other two writers, but the context of his writing is such that he can function effectively in it *now* and he can gain confidence and find his way around the material before the pressures become greater. At that time his purpose will be different, and he may look upon the bus time-table as something relevant to his earlier purpose but not so relevant now.

By the very fact of his being in school the schoolboy writer is facing pressures which he may not find outside. The next collection of writing shows some of the problems which can arise when the pupil is constrained to write in a particular style in which he is not comfortable. We need to consider the nature of these constraints, and here we shall look particularly at two styles of writing often demanded of pupils.

These three pieces make demands upon the pupils' imagination, and then ask for the shaping of the imagined into a story or poem.

18 Ghosts

BACKGROUND The class asked for some more 'special' work. The majority of them appeared to have stories they wanted to write rather than being set a definite topic by me. One or two, however, wanted some sort of lead. I therefore suggested I told them a story and they each told (wrote) me one in return. My story concerned a character who passed through two very different emotions. I emphasized this point afterwards, suggesting their stories might benefit if they paused to dwell on and describe emotions or changes of mood. Some situations where this would be possible were suggested, but not many children used them.

One day a boy named John came home from and he was exhausted weary and whirling in a dream, he just flopped into the armchair and just then he saw a note on the shelf saying his mum will be home at five oclock instead of half past four so he would have to wait an extrar half hour for his tea. So he just flopped back the chair again and fell into a deep sleep. While he was asleep he dreamtd that he heard somthing creaking and he looked at the kitchen door opening and closing then there was arattling sound it was his mother and rushed at the door, and opened it for his mother. he told his mother all about it and lived happily ever after.

Boy *aged 11*

19 Picture

BACKGROUND They were given pictures, generally in colour and largely taken from magazines and of a very varied nature, and given very carefully chosen instructions: 'Try to imagine yourself in this picture in any way you find possible, then write of your experiences within this situation.'

I am the owner of this colourful cart. The cart is getting ready for a fair, pocaing as a gippsee cart. This is the last thing that I am painting that is stood on the sawing horses. The cart is a four wheeler brightly painted in red and yellow and green and gold. On the front of the cart there is a step ladder to get up to the front door and two night lanterns hanging out. The thing that I am painting is the shafts that the horse fits in.

Girl *aged 11*

20 Sound

BACKGROUND The class was asked to write a poem about talking about silence, listening while they were being silent to sounds in and out of the class, considering whether it is ever silent and where one is most likely to find silence, etc.

There is a lot of noise around us
it is the loud things that are nesances
There is always noise around us.

In the country what diffrance
in th country it is quieter we don't
here so much noise how nice it
is to be quiet in the country.

I would be nice if there was
not all those noises we here.

Girl *aged 11*

We might ask ourselves first whether these children really had a story to tell at all. How much experience of stories and poems had they had? The writers were perhaps attempting sophisticated tasks without the raw material on which to build. The writer of 'Ghosts', for example, was trying hard to build up suspense; perhaps he could do it if he were 'talking the story', but suspense-building in writing demands considerable skill.

So how can we help these children? First of all they need a definite stimulus to the imagination; the sort of stimulus provided by an exciting task, a task in which the writer has become wholly involved. And we cannot expect involvement just by the teacher saying in effect 'Get involved'. Such involvement can only come by a long process of 'playing around' with the ideas, with the feelings. The process may be shortened if the child has a background of such 'playing around' through his own reading. For too many children experience of stories is limited to those they heard before the age of about seven; reading for pleasure is not a natural activity for them, and the liveliness of imagination which is stimulated by putting oneself into someone else's story is denied them.

But even when the imagination is lively as a result of contact with exciting and varied literature it is not always possible to produce a story or poem to order. There can have been very few satisfying stories or poems produced by writers who did not definitely *want* to write; satisfaction for a reader primarily comes through the meeting with the writer via the words, and the writer will not be seen in the words unless first the writer has put himself there. A very large proportion of the imaginative or speculative writing quoted earlier in this book was produced by children who wrote first for their own satisfaction – they wanted to write so they wrote – and secondly as a school task. It may be argued against this viewpoint that there will be children who will never want to write at all. We would want to ask, in answer to this, whether the child gains anything from writing a story or poem without really wanting to. If this sort of writing activity is valuable, as we are sure it is, then we see the teacher's task as helping the child to want to write, by encouraging the sort of environment in which writing is a perfectly natural activity.

Illustrative of another type of constraint induced by an insistence on writing in a particular style is the following, which can be left to the reader with no further comment.

21 Measuring the Surface Area of Animals

Place your speciment (the most suitable of which being a small rodent) onto a piece of paper, not required for further use after the experiments completion, but still sufficiently clean as to cause no arm to the mammal. Mark with a single straight line the point at which the naimal's body tapers away to form the animal's tail. After removing from the paper your specimen cut along this line, and disregard as waste the piece of paper which has been cut away. Return to the paper your animal, and carefully bend the paper till it completely encircles the mammal, also record in some way the length of paper necessary in order to completely encircles a single time the mammal. Cut away the remaining paper, and you will find yourself left with a piece of papar roughly equal to the total surface area of your original mammal.

By now weighing the animal, and dividing rhe animal's weight into its surface area, results of use in later experiments may be obtained.

Boy *aged 10*

Finally here is June, a twelve-year-old girl in a remedial stream. We give the context and two pieces of writing, which illustrate many of the difficulties touched on earlier. On the other hand, we can see also her development over a period of approximately four months.

22 Why did they build Stonehenge?

BACKGROUND Following class suggestions as to why Stonehenge should have been built, each pupil wrote about what he considered to be the best suggestions.

On 21st June the sun set rised on mound. And they built Stonehenge, so that they could worship the sun.

On 21st Dec the sun setted on the mountain. And that's the shortest day of the year. On June 21st the sun first risings and on Dec 21st the sun dies. They done this to find out which is the longest day of the year and to find out the shortest day of the year.

The Middle Stone at Stonehenge is called The Altar Stone, perhaps men were killed there, to please the Sun God. Round Stone-henge there are many holes with bones in them.

23 Early English Craftsmen

BACKGROUND Following a class reading from *Then and There* and *Prehistoric Britain*, the pupils wrote about the flint miner's job having the books with them.

A flint miner.

A chalk lamp was very good to use in the dark, they were made out of chalk. Thay lit the lamp and when the smoke started coming out it was alright.

It was many days of hard digging before the flint miners found the layer of flint that they were looking for.

If he had not been told, he might have tipped the precious load down the old sheft with the chalk rubble! The little girl was hauling up the sacks one by one. They dig down and down to the best flint and then they made the best flint into Axes. Flint is very black and shiny.

They dig and dig to the bottom or about 9 feet or ten feet deep and then they dug and dugbut left a long post on their way because if you didn't leave that there they would get closed in.

24 British and Romans

BACKGROUND Following some readings by the teacher the children wrote about what they had heard.

The Romans were to protect themselfs with a hat which had flaps. And a feather at one side.

One day in the year 55BC. And the fight was over to save there queen or something. The British had to save there queen or they would be executed one by one. So the British decided to fight the romans. But the english did not have any protection. So they decided to make catorpaults and javelins and slings. So the British started the war one night and there was dead bodys all around before the fight was over at the beginning there was 90,000 Romans and 8,942. But now there was only 700 Romans and 8,042 and the British had won and the Romans had lost and surrendered.

25 Vikings

BACKGROUND Following the pupils' own individual reading of a chapter from 'Saxons and Vikings'.

what kind of people were the Vikings?
The Vikings were cruel and tourched there prisoners and they killed and slaughtered the mums and children. they pocked them with spears and they also were very good craftsmen, for they carved there own boats and ships.

what bad qualities did they have?
They killed women and children and they tossed the children on
the end of there spear. they also use to kill animals and they
also use to kill anyone they saw.
what good things can you say about them?
The good thing about the vikings is that they made the lovely
ships and they were very good drawers. The viking boat is
called a dragon boat and it is built of ash wood and its length
is 78ft a togethller depth 6ft 9ins and beam 16ft 7ins and that
is what the boats with depth length width

26 I'm going to war

BACKGROUND Following a class reading of a Viking poem, and some discussion
of it.

Im going to war
To fight the poor the old the young
this is my song.
Ishall kill whoever I see
Ah there is land in front of me
I am here to kill I am here to fight
I shall who evers in sight.
I am in a ship of green yellow as well
To go with the sea.
I can't wait to see, my person to kill
I am so blood thirsty, do what i will.
I'm going to kill
I'm going to kill.

Part Six
Contexts

We have looked at many pieces of writing in relation to the activities and processes involved, to purposes, to tasks set, to problems and possibilities. This section presents a variety of pieces set more fully in the contexts in which they were written. We include accounts of the teacher's purposes and roles and in some cases there are transcripts of classroom discussion. In each section the teacher responsible for the work has introduced and commented upon it; this is the work of particular teachers and pupils and particular working situations. What they all seem to reveal is the complexity of the relationship between talking, reading and writing.

In reading these pieces of work in context, questions are raised. How often is the work situation genuinely supportive of the individual writer's efforts? How often is there classroom attention to writing as a process as well as a finished product? Is there a possibility of group discussion and editing of draft copies? How much self-initiated writing is there in school? Does the context enable each writer to find his own way of relating what is new to what is known? How much time is there for writing which sifts, orders and shapes for the purposes of the individual as well as making known to the teacher that what is required has been done? Does the writer feel that he has an audience whose response goes beyond that of the examiner?

We feel that the following contexts *are*, in their individual ways, supportive of the pupils involved. The questions still remain.

Crane Park

Compiled by John Hedgeland

One October morning a class of fourth-year primary children visited the local park. The park is a bit of a wilderness in places, and on this morning mist hung over the diminutive 'River' Crane which runs through it. The children had come well prepared with wellington boots and raincoats, dipping nets and containers, paints, paper and pencils, charcoal and chalks – and they looked and walked and talked. Some of them paddled in the Crane, looked at the bed of the stream through the shallow water, stirred up the mud, gravel and silt, or explored the banks. And all the time, of course, they talked as they explored. During the last century there had been a gunpowder mill in the park, and as they explored some of them speculated (with the lack of hesitation which is characteristic of their age) about how things must have been.

1

A: . . . and I've found out a lot about this up here. There used to be two mills up here. Where that tunnel's caving in you can see the marks where the old – mm – mill, the mill-turner used to be.

A: Yeah, and there's a great big old horse-chestnut tree there.

TEACHER: I see.

C: I'm going to write about it.

B: So really, to have been there it should have been – could have been – over the other side.

D: So there was two mills – either side.

E: All the tunnel there's caved in.

A: You can see the roof's coming through there.

F: Looks as though the mill was there, Jimmy.

G: Where they – mm – you know – where they've been taken away, and there's only the bit where the water runs down and it's . . .

A: [*interrupts*] There's more over there – where the water used to run out from. There's some more ridges [runnels] over there but they're all dried up.

So they went on for several minutes, trying to shape the very minimal signs that they could see (of what might have been the mill site) into a pattern which fitted with how they felt the old powder mill probably was.

When they were not talking, exploring or collecting, some chose to write, some to sketch the way the sunlight slanted down through the clearing mist between the trees, or to make bark rubbings and leaf rubbings, some tried to catch in paint the colour and movement of the water.

Raymond, a boy who had been queried for autism and who for years had struggled with a severe speech defect and an intense feeling of failure listened, sketched a tree (with considerable skill) and busied himself proudly with his responsibility for carrying the class bucket – a hopeful receptacle for large watery specimens. This made him an important member of the group, and when he returned to school he savoured the onerous difficulties which he had overcome by producing his very first piece of entirely original writing.

2

I was the boy who carried the bucket

The sentence was a vast achievement for Raymond, who returns from each school holiday (and sometimes even a weekend!) as a non-reader.

Eventually the children talked their way back to school, and the things they had seen and done became a springboard for a whole host of activities: more talking, printing, drawing, identifying and classifying specimens, setting up a fresh water aquarium, reading, collage making, pressing and mounting, displaying, making friezes, making books and zig-zag folders . . . and so the list continues with each child finding his own way of responding to what seemed important to him, out of the morning's activity. It had been a shared experience and the children's responses were shared – all that they produced was, as always, mounted and displayed for all to enjoy and discuss and reminisce or argue over. The pieces of writing which follow are short extracts from the books, booklets, friezes and displays, and – in the case of three girls – the music which they produced. They give a glimpse of the variety of directions in which the children responded in writing to what seemed individually important to each of them.

3 Crane Water

The water flowed past me clear and smooth, shallow in places. Suddenly the water went dark as it went through a shadow of a tree   it was like going through a tunnel. I placed my hand in the water and made it ripple, a rock copied me and made the water ripple   we had both spoiled the smoothness.

Helena

4 Water

The mirror like sheild of the water was brocken by the wind rippling it. Then again the clear cool mirror was there again. Then walking up the riverside we looked again at the water   but here the water was much much different. The water was rippling in little streams as though the river didn't like me and was frowning at me.

Colin

5 Autumn Day

Some were brown, some were all holes, some were all weins, some were crisp, they were curly, they were orange, red and patches of green. The park was hot and covered in wonderful colours. Twigs dropped off trees as leaves flickered donw, the air was filled with the smell of autumn burning and the smell of dying leaves. Then all of a sudden there was a rustle the leaves were thrown over me I forced myself to throw back   there was laughter. I rolled and kicked   then all of a sudden there was silence. I turned and walked on.

Patricia

6 River Life

Gnats

Gnats are a nuisance. You can even get gnat bites that are very painful. If you kill one and look at it under a microscope it looks big and horrid.

[PICTURE OF A GNAT SEEN UNDER MICROSCOPE]

In hot countries if a gnat gave you a bite it is *very* painful. Gnats go under trees so if you walk under a tree you have to duck.

Fish

River fish need weed. If you have river fish and you put them in a tank they need a sertan hight of water. If they do not have weed they dont get in nufe oxegen and they will drown and sink to the botom.

[PICTURE OF A FISH LOOKING SMILINGLY AT A PIECE OF WEED]

Some weed is very deadly to fish but the curly weed is all right.

Denise

7 Leaves

The leaves flutter down. I kick them up in the air and they come tumbling down and land for everybody   then the park keeper burns them up and they crackle and die out.

[ACCOMPANYING MONTAGE OF MULTI-COLOURED LEAF-PRINTS]

Lynn

8 Crane Park

A leaf fluttered down,
It was joined by another,
They both added to a crisp crackling
Carpet of leaves.
I shuffled through them,
It sounded like a train
Chugging slowly into a station.
I looked up
I heard a funny noise,
It was a squirrel that scurried swiftly
Across the delicate branches.
I stopped for a moment
At my feet I saw large spiky green shells,
I opened one
Inside was a shining brown conker
It reminded me of a jewel.
I tripped and rolled
Over and over in the leaves.
They felt prickly and uncomfortable,
I could smell burning fires
In the distance.

Wendy

9 Things of Autumn

The leaves crackled as I trod and it made a sound like a wave breaking on
the seashore. Leaves fluttered down. Some twirled and others whirled and
some spun to the ground. The sun gleamed through the trees and in the
distance we saw a bonfire with hazy smoke rising up. There was a lovely
smell coming from it. The smell of dry burnt up leaves. It was nice and
pleasant and all was calm and peaceful.

Sandra

10 Leaves

Twirling leaves falling,
Twisting to and fro,
Into the air,
Like a breaking wave
A colourful blanket,
Waiting to be burnt.

More and more fall,
Curling round and round,
Crackling, crunching,
Troddne to the ground.
Soon the trees are bare,
All the leaves are gone.

Lorraine

11 Water

The quite water ran past. Dark green weed had to cling to the stony and
sandy river bed. There were white patches where the river catches on a
twig. The water was wet and dirty.

Carol

12 Autumn Today

Today is peaceful,
Today is quiet,
Today heavey dew is on the ground,
Today theres mist that clears away,
Today is cold when you go outside,
Today the leaves are damp and still,
Today is Autumn.

Colin

13 Oak

Oak trees grow in parks and woods. Squirrels peel the acorn and eat the
seed to save up for the winter. But pigeons eat the holl acorn. This is a
leave off of a Oak tree.

[PICTURE AND RUBBING OF AN OAK LEAF]

Deborah

14 Pond Life

Pond Insects

I was looking at this creature when its body was moving a lot, then white
eggs started to come out. At first she laid in fours later she laid in three's.
The black dots on her back are beginning to close into a big black shape.
She laid roughly an inch of eggs. When I put the creature into the big pot
the eggs stuck to the container they were laid in. She took about thirty
minutes to lay her eggs.

[DETAILED DRAWING OF THE CREATURE]

Fishes

This is a fish catch in Crane Park

[DETAILED PICTURE OF FISH]

Its back tail can spread out about 1/8″. Its 1½″ long. The fin on its back can spread about 1/8″. I cut the dead fish open and black stuff came out. Here is a picture of the inside.

[PICTURE]

Its name is a minnow.

Carole

15 Autumn

The Autumn fire burns the crackling leaves,
A leaf flutters down from the trees,
Whirling, spinning, swirling,
The ground is covered with
Red, orange, yellow, brown,
These are the Autumn colours.
Crunch! crunch, crunch,
I tread on some leaves,
Crisp and golden.

16 Crane Life

[PICTURE OF PLANARIA]

The name of this creture is Planaria lugubrio wich I looked at with a magnifine glass   it sticks to the botom and slowly moves.

Ian

17 Water Mites

Water mites are funny creatures and are quite coulerful. There is one and it is called an hydrarachina globosa wich is a very funy name and is female. And runs around in ponds and streams and pools of mud.

[PICTURE OF WATER-MITE]

Mostly these are attached to water bugs abd beetles and they are very hard to get of because they have little pinchers on there legs.

Lynda

18 The Lime Tree

The lime tree is also known as the linden. The bark of the tree is rough and not very straight.

[RUBBING]

This is a bark rubbing from a lime tree

The seed from the lime tree is a circular nut which is a yellowish-brown colour and covered with very fine hairs. The tree will grow to the height of about one hundred and thirty feet high and the trunk about fourteen feet in circumference. The lime tree mainly grows in park's and avenue's and sometimes it grows in people's gardens. The bark of the lime tree is mainly used for carving as it is very easily cut.

[SKELETON LIME LEAF]

This is the remainder from a skeleton leaf. If you look closely you can see the small veins. This leaf comes from the lime tree

[LIME LEAF RUBBING]

This is a leaf rubbing which comes from a lime tree.
The veins on this leaf go up it in pairs. The leaf itself is a rounded shape and meets at a point at the top.

Wendy

19 Leaves

I kicked my way through the leaves,
A crisp and crackly sound it was,
The leaves flew up into the air
as I kicked them,
A leaf was spinning downwards
Another leaf came down heading straight,
I rolled in a pile of leaves,
They prickled my bare skin
and stuck to my clothes.
I got up and started walking,
As I looked ahead smoke was swirling upwards,
Burning the leaves.

Kim

20 Autumn Leaves

Intro:

block:

The Au-tumn waves are ve-ry bright,

You can see them whir-ling twir-ling down. They

flu-tter and glide as they tumble down,

All the Au-tumn col-ours whir-ling round.

v.2   Autumn's another world it is,
A world of colourful Autumn leaves,
A whirl, a twirl, a flutter of leaves,
Look upon this Autumn Day.

Julius Caesar

Compiled by Nick Levine

The secondary-school student has a tough job in coping with the varying writing demands made on him; he may be asked to express himself in his own style and words, to adopt the style and words of the particular subject specialist (however alien that may be in terms of his everyday language), or to do something between the two. It may be that it would be less confusing for the student either to do his own thing or to be presented with clear models of specialist style and language and be drilled so that with enough practice the required style and language would become habitual.

But perhaps it is not as clear-cut as that: perhaps the student's everyday language *is* inappropriate to the teacher's purpose in asking for the writing if an element of that purpose is to give practice in using specialist words, or to give practice in taking an impersonal stance for which an impersonal style is needed; and the student's purpose, too, may be to gain new control and new skills through being able to adopt this new stance and use these new words. On the other hand the student may, in trying to master not only new knowledge but also new specialist words and new styles, suffer from intellectual indigestion or utter confusion: the specialist words may be a barrier to his understanding and the alien stance may be so difficult to adopt that he switches off completely.

The following pieces of writing reflect these dilemmas. The language and style are a compromise between personal and impersonal writing, between the words of the individual writer and historicalese.

The writing also reflects my attitude to History teaching. I believe that History is a matter of 'I wonder why . . .', 'I wonder what it was like to . . .', and 'What do *you* think . . .?' So at many points in my teaching I try to provide enough colourful and accurate detail for students to be able to enter into situations, be present imaginatively at past events, form opinions that are not too superficial on matters of doubt, and decide where they stand on matters of controversy. Did Caesar deserve to die is such a point of controversy. To form any kind of judgement on the matter the student has to understand something of what Caesar did and to consider and make explicit some of his own thoughts on the conflicting claims of enlightened despotism and democracy. In one sense Caesar is distant in time, in space, in life style, and in attitudes; yet factual knowledge about Caesar can interest, can involve, and can be used in an active and 'immediate' way. My purpose in the classes that led up to the written assignment and in asking for the writing in the form that I did was to set up a situation in which the students consolidated their knowledge about Caesar in such a way that the writer was personally involved in, and enjoyed, what he was doing.

The preparation for the written assignment was as follows: first was a lesson in which I presented the students with, and they wrote down, a list of twenty things that Caesar did; some were elaborated on, either because I foresaw a possible source of confusion or in response to a question, and some were simply copied down. Then came a lesson in which individuals argued from one or two of the things that Caesar did that he should, or should not, have been killed, and others tried to counter these arguments either from other things that Caesar did or from their own attitudes and experience. Finally there was a class reading from the scene in *Julius Caesar* in which Brutus and Antony are pleading with the Rome crowd, a digression–discussion of crowd behaviour, and the watching of a ten-minute extract from the film *Julius Caesar* which, although crackly and indistinct, was strong on the atmosphere at the time of the murder.

The written assignment was that the class should write a speech attacking or defending Caesar. I asked them to try to use a variety of evidence in support of their cases, not just one or two pieces.

The class was an able, streamed class in their second year at a comprehensive school. Here are three of the 'speeches' that were written.

1 Julius Caesar

Friends, Caesar was a great man. These people made him a tyrant only in their minds. Just because he took the government from them they are mad with him. Hatred fills them. They do not know what they have done, his death was for an unworthy cause.

He expanded our empire. He made us stronger our name is muttered almost everywhere because of him. We are an almighty nation because of him and him only. His word was right and just. He faced his death bravely not like that cursed Brutus. Brutus whould have shied away like a little dog, if he knew his death was coming.

He gave the poor a life that was worth living, he gave them jobs that would help them financially. He stopped tax farming that meant a much fairer life for everybody.

It wasn't himself that made Caesar dictator it was us and it was us that made him a dictator for life. So you can't say that he made himself what he was and deprived us of our government, because we took the choice and gave him our answer he was to be dictator over us.

Also debtors are given a longer time to pay how fairer could you get. Many of us have been in this predicament and what a blessing this new rule is.

His will said we had land of his and other things of his possessions. How kind and thoughtful was our Caesar we were his main thoughts and how he loved us. He did not deserve to die.

2 Caesar Should've Lived

Friends, Romans, countrymen, lend me your ears, Caesar has been murdered. Our ruler, our dictator, stabbed to death by his own senate. Why should he've died in this way? Did he not help all of us? Did he not bring in reforms? Did he not give land to the poor? Did he not employ the poor, did he not give debtors longer to pay. Did he not build many large cities, great cities. Did he not protect the poor from slave labour. Did he not give us great feasts. Why did he have to die? He was a just man. Did he not expand the Roman Empire. Did he not lead Rome in many battles and we did come out victorious. He was a great tactian. Oh why did he have to die? I'll tell you, it's because the senate were scared of him, frightened, terrified. They called him a tyrant and other ridiculios things. They were jealous of his great rule, his kingdom. They murdered him cowardly. The circumstances were like a whole Roman legion onto a small village.

He died bravely, he fought until his best friend, yes even Brutus, stabbed him with the others. He gave no more resistance. He died a bloody death. Caesar our beloved.

HAIL CAESAR.

3 Caesar deserved to die

Rejoice! People of Rome and it's great Empire! Caesar is dead. You are free at last from that tyrant, Caesar. The people of Rome can once again rule their city and land; decide for themselves whether they should send their sons into battle. Never again will there by such a tyrant leading Rome. Never again will one man decide laws.

Caesar was a friend to me and I to him, but I could never agree with his way of thought in law. Oh, yes Caesar did give some land to the poor, but what are you to the better when your sons are taken away from it to bloody wars?? What use is land without workers? Any fool could see he was just trying to be popular. And why didn't you see? Caesar was teaching you not to think; not to question his laws; not to think of the Empire as a whole, but to think of your own small piece. In fact to think like him. To think selfishly when a whole Empire is at stake is criminal. Caesar thought self-ishly. He was a dictator: his word was the last word. He used his power in the wrong way. Why, because Caesar was dictator should he judge legal cases himself? How could a man make a law completely of his own will without consulting anyone else, let alone the people who it affected? Caesar was like our master and we his slave. He could treat us any way he chose. He could consult us, or he could chose not to. Caesar chose not to. We feel as a slave feels when his master takes away his old tunic and pre-sents him with a new one that doesn't fit and the master refuses to listen to his pleas.

Caesar did too much with his power. He treated it in the way of a small child; he did too much with it. He too far. He made himself a God and put his statue in the temples for us to worship. He put his head on our coins.

Why do think we Romans voted for self-government? To save us from a dictator's selfish rule. When a dictator rules it is natural that we should protest. When Caesar took no notice of our pleas, what could we do to get rid of him? It is unfortunate that it had to be death, but it was the only way.

Do not weep, Romans, at a tyrant's death; look forward to a pleasant future.

The reader may like to consider different purposes from the ones implicit in these extracts, and their implications for the language a student might have used to state the facts about, or speculate on the reasons for, Caesar's death. Clearly the purposes and the language are, at bottom, inextricable.

Revamping the lamp ?

Compiled by Nick Levine

The class was a class of thirty-three students working towards O-level History, most of the students being likely to scrape through with a bit of luck, some to do well, some to fail. There were pressures of time such that Florence Nightingale was only 'worth' an hour; and an aim of that hour was to have the students able to write about the 'Character, career, and importance of Florence Nightingale' in a quarter of an hour and in such a way that some examiner is going to tick frenziedly as he reads.

Let us accept the situation as read and tackle the question of how to achieve the aim. As the teacher I assumed that it was not possible for the students to write without being at some point interested in Florence Nightingale as a person. I think it is true to say that writing a fluent and relevant essay depends on having something to say and that this in turn is hardly possible unless the writer's interest has shaped and used the material at some time before the act of writing. Even if the final spur to an act of writing is an examination paper, it is not that which determines what is written or how. It may determine what is selected as relevant to a particular question; it may dictate a particular style of writing that is thought to impress an examiner, and it may discourage speculation and exploration. But it does not influence what is in the writer's mind that he can draw on; that has been decided much earlier. Thus the nature of the meeting between the student and the material he will ultimately write about will greatly influence how he writes. In the case of Florence Nightingale I had not the resources of money, materials or imagination to make this first meeting other than a matter of teacher-talk and student-listen. The class textbook was criminally dull on the subject, mainly because it was lacking in the kind of detail that makes the reader want to read on; other books were distortingly sloppy, too sophisticatedly debunking or too long. Here, then, are some extracts from a transcript of that lesson.

TEACHER: Right. We're going to do Florence Nightingale. Can you take the notes in rough, what you think's worth putting down.

Florence, now she came from a nice rich Hampshire family, except that she wasn't like her parents and others had expected because apparently she found parties boring and was, from very young, serious, dedicated; in other words, she must have had one of these beliefs from pretty early that she knew what she wanted to do, and what she wanted to do was to nurse. Now this may not sound very unusual or special but in those days it was, because nurses generally were a very boozy lot . . . It was a rough profession – not the sort of profession that *nice* young ladies from *nice* families went into.

Florence Nightingale appears to have been something like this: this is what somebody said when she was thirty-four: 'She is tall, very slight, willowy in figure; she has thick shortish rich brown hair, very delicate colouring, grey eyes which are generally pensive and drooping, but when they close can be the merriest eyes I ever saw, and perfect teeth making her smile the sweetest smile I ever saw. . . .

[The quotation continued and was followed by another contemporary's impression of Florence Nightingale and by an account of her career up to 1854.]

STUDENT: When was she born?

TEACHER: 1820.

Right. And then, as you know, comes the Crimean War and this changes things. From what you read yesterday* what would you say were the problems, the health problems, in the Crimea. Can you remember anything?

STUDENTS: Cholera . . . yes . . . dystentery . . . diarrhoea . . . yes . . . scarlet fever . . . (Teacher 'Yes' at frequent points)

TEACHER: Yes. Cholera, dysentery, diarrhoea, the lot. Don't know that scurvy's mentioned . . . all sorts of things. Now, one of her friends, who had the unfortunate name of Sidney Herbert . . .

STUDENTS: (cackle)

TEACHER: . . . was at this time Secretary at War and Secretary at War was the top politician back in England that runs the war, we haven't got an equivalent now. Anyway, Sidney Herbert wrote asking her whether she would take some nurses to the Crimea. [The lesson contined with an account of her arrival at Scutari hospital.]

Here's what somebody says at the time: 'The magic of her power over men was felt in the room where operations took place. There perhaps the maimed soldier, if not yet resigned to his fate, might be craving death rather than meet the knife of the surgeon, but when such a one looked and saw that the honoured Lady-in-Chief was patiently standing beside him with lips closely set and hands folded, decreeing herself to go

---

* Duplicated extracts from Russell's *Dispatches from the Crimea*.

through the pain of witnessing pain, he used to fall into the mood of obeying her silent command, and finding strange support in her presence bring himself to submit and endure.' So she did offer some help at the operations level. She also wandered round the wards with the lamp – thus The Lady With The Lamp – and this is different from earlier nurses, who, if they had them, would have retired quietly with their bottle of whatever it was and drunk themselves into a stupor. Florrie was a non-drinker and this was rare among nurses at the time. When she got to the main hospital at Scutari – there's the Crimea, that's the Black Sea, there's Constantinople, there's Scutari, it's a long way from the Crimea that's the bit at the top of the Black Sea. Scutari's a long way across the Black Sea, two hundred odd miles, that's the main army hospital there – when she got there the death rate was 42 per cent and they were beginning to get a terrific flood of casualties from the winter of 1854. Do you remember that bit in the passage, I hope you do, about the winter, and the effects of it?

STUDENTS: Yes ... yes ...

TEACHER: Right, now, that is quite something, 42 per cent death rate and a vast hospital network with about twelve thousand men in it; and this is the problem she faced when she got there. It was utterly utterly squalid; and so the side of her that has been stressed in later biographies is the less romantic one ... she got busy scrubbing.

STUDENTS: [Laughter and ribald comment]

TEACHER: You won't believe it but that wasn't intentional. Right, anyhow, she slowly and busily got the place clean and a side of her that again is not mentioned in all the books is that she was a real pushing little Madam. She got things done by writing and pressurizing and making herself a nuisance which are very admirable qualities in the circumstances. She flooded back letters to friend Sidney Herbert here. One of the results of this was that she got a sanitary Commission set up looking at the sanitation. For example, cholera, which is one of the killer diseases, is water-borne. Cholera is the result of the sewage system getting muddled with the drinking system, and that was very, very much happening in the hospital so that the sanitary Commission found things were foul and began to redrain the hospitals and improve the water supply. That's one thing which she got done. She got the wards scrubbed, that's another thing.

OK and she also sent back for public help; she publicized her needs through Russell and *The Times*; she publicized her needs. Things like balaclavas and cardigans, all these lovely clothing names after people involved in the Crimea, and soap and carbolic and scrubbing brushes –

and all sorts of other cleansing things. Now, to cut a fairly long story short the death rate in Scutari dropped from 42 per cent to 2 per cent. Wowee ... that is a *staggering* drop. Forty-two per cent to 2 per cent. Mainly, it is true, not from the nursing but probably from improved sanitation, but partly also from better nursing and better care. And one other thing she was good at – she was concerned with ventilation. She used to build her hospitals with small separate wards because she believed in maximum ventilation. And another thing she believed in was the sort of welfare of the patients; therefore she believed in books and recreation rooms. She does seem to have driven herself quite fantastically hard. For example, there is evidence that she was up frequently twenty-four hours on end, and she wrote countless letters, organizing, and to judge by some of the rude things said about her by the male officers, she made herself a thorough pest to them in Scutari. She was really a very busy woman. Now, after her work in Scutari she went to the Crimea and set up a number of field hospitals actually near the battle area. Then she returned.

The lesson continued in much the same vein to her death in 1910, ending with thirty seconds consideration of why she was important, before the bell went.

These extracts raise many questions. Was it wise, for example, to ask the students to make their own notes? Would it have been wiser to suggest that they just listen? Or should they have received notes already duplicated? Which of these three would best ensure their understanding, their recall of events in Florence Nightingale's life and their ability to assess her importance in the Crimea, to nursing, or as an influence in changing the status of women? In fact what happened was that the speed of delivery varied according to my assessment of importance: this was taken up in their initial note-taking such that some sections of the lesson (e.g. her influence during operations) were omitted by all and some sections (e.g. the drop in death-rate from 42 per cent to 2 per cent) were noted by all. But this does not answer the question as to how vital the note-taking was in terms of their understanding. And did the particular style of the teacher help them because it was fairly relaxed and the language fairly non-specialist, or did it hinder because the students were given too little guidance as to what they should note down and were, in fact, left to decide what was noteworthy? Answers, even tentative ones, must wait until some of the notes have been seen.

The next stage in the student's writing–understanding process was for them to write up the notes. I suggested that they could organize their rough notes into those concerned with character, with career, and with importance. Here are some of these notes.

2 Florence Nightingale 1820-1910

She came from a rich Hampshire family. She found life boring and from very young she was dedicated to nursing. She was very cheerfull and very dedicated. Because she was wealthy she could spend many of her years travelling through Europe looking at hospitals. In 1851 at the age of 31 she spent 3 months in a German hospital at Kaiserworth. In 1853 she was main lady for sick ladies at an institute. She had a friend Sidney Herbert who was secretary of war wrote to Florence asking her if she would take a team of nurses into the Crimea. At the same time she wrote to him asking if she could go out to the Crimea. So she went out to the Crimea with 38 nurses and a lot of supplies: she got out there and was a tremendous help, men found courage on the operating table when she was present. Also when she got to the main hospital at Scutari when she got there the death rate was 42% and they were beginning to get a terrific flood of casualties from the terrible winter of 1854. There were 12,000 casualties in it. When she got there the place was in a shambles, but she persevered in cleaning the place up. The way she get what she wanted by flooding letters to important people like Sidney Herbert until she got what she wanted done. eg she got a santary inspection set up. Through Russell she got what she wanted by the TIMES publishing her needs in Britain eg she wanted sweaters, barcolics, balaclavas, blankets. After she got there the death rate dropped from 42% to 2% which is a staggering. She believed in well ventilated wards. After Scutari she set up field hospitals at the front and when the war was over she returned to Scutari and refused to leave until every British (wounded) soldier had been taken away. She was the last to leave and in 1856 she returned to England to a royal welcome. But in 1857 she collapsed from ill health from the Crimea. From then on she spent much of her life in bed. But she was still active, she got a cammision set up into the health of the troops. This cut the death rate by 50% in the army. She also set up an Army Medical School. In 1860 The Nightingale Nursing School was set up in St Thomas. She then gave advice to countries like India on their health system and in 1906 she got the Order of Merit. She ended her life in 1910 at the age of 90.

Michael *aged 15*

It is interesting to speculate why confusions creep into notes and the answers would be myriad and would certainly include inadequacies of the particular lesson and factors like the six earlier 'periods' in the day, the lunch and its digestive consequences, and what life was like at home. But it is even more pertinent to wonder about the good understandings. Unless one believes that teacher-talk or print-on-the-page becomes understood in some mystical or inevitable way one has to consider the process by which it is understood and one has to assume that it is an active process on the part of the learner. A definition of 'learning' that implies passiveness on the learner is, I suspect, psychological nonsense. So the notes should not be looked at in terms of the 'emasculation' or contraction of a lesson, but as individual attempts to take over, and make their own, certain facts and ideas first met during a lesson.

A closer look at Michael's notes, for example, reveals just this. 'Because she was wealthy she could spend many of her years travelling through Europe' is his inference from the lesson which stated that she came from a rich family and, later, that she travelled widely. 'Men found courage on the operating table when she was present', is his effective summary of a rather 'difficult' contemporary's account. '. . . she persevered in cleaning the place up' focuses on a strong feature of her character, but the word 'persevere' does not appear in the lesson. '. . . at the front . . .', and '. . . royal welcome . . .' express certain facts better than the lesson did, though one cannot know whether he intended 'royal welcome' to imply both that Victoria and Albert met her and that she was popularly acclaimed. Sometimes his attempts to make the information his own are not so successful. His use of 'in a shambles' is less satisfactory to describe the nature of Scutari hospital when she arrived than the lesson's 'squalid'. And I suspect that when he uses 'sanitary inspection' he understands something quite different from 'Sanitary Commission' – he is, in fact, one of the school's few boarders.

The sentences are short, as one would expect in notes, but one can see that the shortness has not precluded some thoughtful writing. Thus, '. . . in 1856 she returned to England to a royal welcome. But in 1857 she collapsed from ill health from the Crimea. From then on she spent much of her life in bed. But she was still active . . .' shows a good understanding. In an unthinking contraction of the lesson these 'buts' would have got lost.

A fascinating feature of these notes and the ones which follow is the degree to which the personality of each individual emerges. Yet the lesson itself was 'common' and the knowledge of Florence Nightingale that they brought to that lesson was minimal, for most of them merely an impression of a saintly young thing drifting through dark smelly wards with a smile and a lamp. The differences in their notes certainly cannot be put down to differences of prior knowledge. Do the differences, then, reflect an externally imposed expectation, or are they an outward sign of *how* understanding happens? I think it is the latter, and if I'm right the implications for much secondary-school writing are enormous. It would mean, for example, that for the students to have time and opportunity to explore a subject in their own language becomes essential; and that to insist that 'History (or Geography or Chemistry or Biology) notes should be written like this' might inhibit and limit understanding. The form of notes would not just be a peripheral matter of technique.

Christopher's and Lesley's notes are perhaps less successful than Michael's. Christopher has a clipped style which sometimes makes it hard to assess the extent of his understanding, and Lesley has not sorted out 'Character, career and importance', though she has got quite an impression of Florence Nightingale and her achievements.

3 Florence Nightingale 1820-1910

She came from a rich Hampshire family. She wanted to nurse from a very young age – a desire.

Because she had money she could travel and went to Europe to see some hospitals. She was employed in a German hospital – Kaiserwerth. Then she returned and went to work in Britain. Then came the Crimean war. Sidney Herbert wrote and asked her if she would take some nurses to the Crimea. She went – with 38 nurses and a lot of supplies. She offers help – operations. Makes rounds with lamp hence Lady and the Lamp. At Scutari the death rate was 42% and they were beginning to get winter casualties. 12,000 casualties there. – She got busy and got the place clean. She wrote to Sydney Herbert and got things done. ie: Sanitary conditions. Water supply, wards scrubbed. Publicised her needs back home. ie: Cardigans, Soap, Carbolic, Balaclavas. The death rate dropped to 2%. She was concerned with ventilation and welfare of patients – Books and recreations. She went to the Crimea and set up field hospitals. She was the last to leave Scutari. King and Queen met her. 1856 1857 she collapsed from ill health. She spent most of her last 53 years in bed. She was responsible for a Royal Commission for the Health of Troops. Death rate of troops in Army halved. Set up School of Medics. Set up (1860) The Nightingale Nursing home at St Thamas's hospital. Advised countries like India to change Health Methods. 1907 awarded the O.M.

Christopher *aged 16*

4 Florence Nightingale

CHARACTER She came from a rich Hampshire home. Parties bored her, she became dedicated she wanted to nurse. Nursing was not the work which young ladies did. She was elegant not pretty, laughed a lot. Because she was wealthy she travelled in Europe. 1851 she was employed for 3 months in a good German. In 1853 she was the Lady Supervisor institute for Gentlewomen. One of her friends Sidney Herbet was Secretary at War. he wrote to her to ask her if she would take a band of 38 nurses to the Crimea. Florence was a non-drinker and had a command over the men. They trusted her.

ACHIEVEMENTS She went to the main hospital at Scutari the death rate was 42%. There were a great many casualties from the winter of 1854. The hospital was very squalid she made the place clean. She got things done by making a nuisence of herself. She sent lots of letters to Sidney Herbet and got a Commission into Sanitation at the hospital. They re-drained and improved water supply. She got wards scrubbed death rate fell from 42% to 2%. Publised her needs through Russell and the Times.

She believed in Welfare of her patients. Went to Crimea set up field hospitals in battle area. Last to leave Scutari – returned as a known person 1856. 1857 collapsed from ill health next 53 years she spent in bed. Still active in setting up Royal Commission in the health of troops. Result death rate of soldiers from disease halfed. Behind first Army Medical School. In 1860 she started Nightingale Nursing home at St Thomas' hospital from large public subscription of £50 000.

IMPORTANCE Advised various countries including India on health system. 1907 awarded O.M. (Order of Merit) 1910 died.

Lesley *aged 15*

So to the last stage; the students were asked to write about 'The Career and Importance of Florence Nightingale' in about twelve minutes, without their notes; they had been forewarned that they would have to write something about Florence Nightingale the following day but had no foreknowledge of the precise assignment. The influences on the students are different now; the writing probably has little or no value to the writers in terms of deepening their understanding; it doesn't usefully inform anyone about Florence Nightingale; it merely helps an assessor to assess, provokes the examiner to tick.

Yet time has passed, and there are many changes in Michael and Christopher's work, in words, in relationships made more, or less, clear, and in their attempts, however faltering, to make statements about Florence Nightingale's importance; and so to make explicit many thoughts they had not written down before.

5 Outline the career and estimate the importance of Florence Nightingale

Florence Nightingale came from a rich Hampshire family. From an early age she wanted to go into nursing. In her late teens she travelled around Europe looking at different hospitals and generally seeing what she thought was best. In 1851 she got an appointment to work at a German hospital at Kaiserworth she worked there 3 months. In 1852 she worked at a lady institute in England. When war broke out, Sydney Herbert who was the Minister of War wrote to her and asked her if she would go out to the Crimea with a squad of nurses. At the same time she wrote to him asking if she could go out. Then she went out to the Crimea with a squad of 38 nurses and hell of a lot of supplies. When she arrived at the main hospital Scutari she was appaled at the conditions. The Wards weren't ventilated propelly, not enough beds, disease spread quick. 3,000 men were at the hospital where she worked and she started getting the placed cleared up. She ventilated the dorms, spaced the beds well and cleaned up the entire place. She did a magnificent job and was a great encouragement to the men. When she got there 42% of the men who entered the hospital died, by the time she left it was down to 2%. She did a magnificent job. Always writing to England asking for balaklaves, soap, blankets. She was one of the last to leave the Crimea and received a heroe welcome when she got back to England. But from the sheer strain she collapsed and spent the rest of her life in bed from the overwork she had done at the Crimea. But she was not ideal in bed, she wrote reports for other governments heath programmes eg Egypt. She was very important she also set up general hospitals. eg St Thomes nursing home. She was recognised all over the world. She organised a commsion into the armies heath standards and the sick rate dropped 50%. She was very important for nursing.

Michael *aged 15*

6 Florence Nightingale

Outline the career and estimate the importance of F.N.

She belonged to a rich family, and so could afford to travel abroad, where she visited hospitals. She was employed for six months in a German hospital, and on returning home, she worked in a hospital for ladies. Sidney Herbert, a friend, asked her, in her capasity of War secretary, if she would go to the Crimea, which she did with 39 other nurses. On arriving at the hospital at Suctari, she scrubbed the place out, after her efforts the death rate dropped from 42% to 2%. Through pressure she put on, where she was, and letters home, she improved things greatly in many ways. This was very important in the saving of lives.

When she arrived home, she became ill and collapsed, but although she stayed in bed for nearly the rest of her life, she still took a part in many things. Health legistration in the army. From money given to her, the St. Thomas hospital trainning school was started. All this was very important for the future.

Christopher *aged 16*

Finally, here are two more passages. The first, an extract, is chosen to show an attempt to come to grips with the problem of deciding what Florence Nightingale's importance was. The second is chosen to remind one of the power of the 'personal' voice, especially in the passion of the final two words.

7

... and she died 1910 at the age of 90.

Her corea was very important, it made nursing a decent corea instead of a corea for bored drunks; she made the death rate of hospital lower than the rate of living people that left hospitals. She raised the status of women by giving them a decent corea. She also started off training homes for nurses, and these nurses were in demand all over the country. She started off a medical service for the army.

She was a very great woman, brave and strong minded changing the corea of nursing and status for women.

Martin *aged 16*

8 Outline the career and estimate the importance of F.N.

F.N. was born to rich parents who tried to bring her up in a proper manner to become a good wife. But F.N. had different ideas and from a very early age showed great dedication to nursing.

It was in 1851 that F.N. went to a hospital in Germany, later to return as as a lady supervisor of the institute for sick and gentle women. A good friend of F.N. was a chap called Sydney Herbert. who wrote to F.N. asking if she could gather up a few dedicated nurses and some supplies and come over to scutari. She did accept and took with her 38 nurses. When she arrived she found the 'hospitals' in an appauling condition and with the help of many pushing letters to Britain she gained, by means of a petition by the many wounded patients a sanitary commission. When this took effect all the hospitals were completed scrubbed out and cleaned and the death rate dropped from 48% to 2% in the time she was there. She then went on to the Crimea where many troops lives were being lost because of desease and she carried on to do the same work there. Two years after she collapsed of ill-health to spend the 53 more years in bed. But this did not stop F.N. she formed a Nightingale nursing home in 1860 and helped many other places in need. In 1907 she was awarded the order of merit and in 1910 she died aged 93.

THE END

Clive *aged 15*

Blood

Compiled by Mike Torbe

If there is a popular conception of science and scientific writing, it involves ideas of impartiality, objectivity, cold statements of observable fact, and detachment from the actual experience itself. In other words, there is no notion of involvement, of a sense of wonder, or even of *passion*. Certainly, if the reaction of our students is a general one, the experience of most pupils is that individuality and involvement are discouraged in the scientific writing they are asked to do at school.

Well: does scientific writing *have* to detach the pupil from his involvement? If he is excited by the wonder of discovery about himself and his environment, why can't he write about his excitement and wonder as well as 'the facts'? Isn't it at least possible that the pupil's learning will be encouraged if he can write about his own involvement, his own delight of discovery, rather than being asked to separate himself from his experience? It may even be that this is a necessary first stage of the actual process of scientific learning; that unless the pupil *is* excited, the writing becomes no more than an imposed, routine, even meaningless task.

We were running an experimental course involving team-teaching of Science and English, attempting to demonstrate the possibilities of combining what might seem unlikely approaches. Since we were teaching College of Education students, some of whom were mature students, and all of whom were non-scientific, the intentions were both to teach, and to suggest to potential Primary teachers ways of teaching. We had already had four weeks, an hour a week, on the course, so the students were fairly well accustomed to our ideas and approaches. On this occasion we began by showing them without comment a loop-film, about two to three minutes long, of the blood defences – white corpuscles attacking a bacterium in a diseased part of the blood. Then, as the film looped round for the second time, the science lecturer began talking about the blood defences, casually, in 'non-scientific' terms. He discussed the four ways the blood defends itself against bacteria, and pointed out on the film the stages of the particular process we were watching; he also answered the students' fascinated questions about other features on the film. By the time he had finished – about ten minutes – he had offered the students a fair amount of solid information about the blood defences, including several important terms – like plasma, capillaries, fibrins, lymphocytes, phagocytes, and so on.

I took over and talked for five minutes or so. I offered for consideration the thought, astonishing enough, that all this was taking place *now*. And then I asked them not to consider this as a purely scientific exercise – 'Discuss the blood defences' – but to try and become absorbed by the sheer wonder of it, to ask themselves what it meant to them, to react not intellectually but emotionally to the film and the talk we'd had from Angus. So would they please write something about the blood defences in any way they liked. And let it be anonymous, too: don't bother to put names on the paper. Here is a selection of the pieces. It seems worth printing eleven of them to give a clear idea of the range of responses.

1

Round and round are body in an everlasting flow,
the blood which is so dear to us, although we may not know;
Red cells, white cells, what's the difference between,
Some would show their ignorance and would never want to know.
Others would be tempted by their curiosity too keen.
Our blood is life and death to us,
Surely that is good enough.
All the bacteria that swims through our blood,
Never really ever does us any good,
Yet it goes on multiplying
We meet the anti-tocsin and the white lymphocytes,
To help us fight a battle and prevent us from dying.

2

When I cut myself this morning I never thought of all the tiny things which make up blood – the physical pain in my finger was all that mattered. The cut was dealt with in some way – it stopped bleeding. I didn't do anything to help it, it functioned completely alone. I suppose now it will go ahead and repair my finger until I have forgotten I ever did it. How many times does this happen? Each time the matter is dealt with quickly efficiently and completely. What happens inside me which is also dealt with in this way and I know nothing of it? To have a knowledge of what white corpuscles do is interesting but seems not to relate to the job that is done so consistantly and continuously in every living animal. To know how the bacteria is eliminated by the blood cells seems far from the total processes of the blood, just one job among many which never stops from day to day.

3

I have a feeling this lecture might worry me later e.g. while I lie awaiting sleep. Am I really such a hive of industry? Or have my corpuscles slowed down to a puny trickle?

Its hard to believe that that red substance I treasure and which has sentimental overtones is in reality a highly mechanised unit. Do the Fibrins worry in case they might be doing more work than Lymphocytes? No productivity deals, just as well. Can one imagine the consequences of such disputes.

4

Every day thousands of deaths take place within my body. A startling thought yet in place of the deaths thousands of births occur. It is a never-ending cycle, and somewhat vicious. The cells become old, no longer function properly, become useless to the body and die. Just like the old people in the world they are useless so they die, and a new birth takes place so that their position can be filled.

But what of the bacteria that enter our bloodstream and organs. Can they be compared to all the evil influences in the world? A brave fight is always put up against the bacteria but as in life battles and wars are often lost and death comes out the victor.

5

We take for granted the functions going on inside the body, as far as we are concerned they don't exist until we are ill and even then we may not understand what is happening. Just think – all those little tiny canables known as blood cells running around your body getting rid of bacteria. Most perculiar feeling . . . When I think of it, I find my head shrinking backwards to rest on my shoulders and my lips curl. To see the functions of one drop of blood magnified on a screen to almost life-size is very dramatic all it needs is deep heavy background music, as the bacteria is isolated!

6

The film strip fascinated me, the white corpuscle circulating around the bacteria as if sizing it up but it did not attack. Maybe that was what the blood had been under a microscope for anyway because the bacteria in some sick person's bloodstream had gained the upper hand. I wish I could see the same film strip over again but this time with a healthy sample of blood and maybe then we could see the interesting sight of bacteria actually under attack.

How lazy and indolent the red blood cells were – staying put, not caring about the danger in their midst, a danger which, if not tackled, could surely in the end endanger their existence.

How fascinating that these two vital roles could be kept so separate from each other and yet at the same time be totally dependent on each other for life.

I wonder how blood looks when life in the person has ceased and may be bacteria has gained the upper hand – would it typify death as aptly as the other typified life?

7

It is difficult to imagine, that such tiny blood cells could protect our bodies so efficiently. How on earth do the white cells manage to keep up their insatiable appetites for bacteria? The whole function of blood is one which is not easily accepted, and of course taken for granted.

When at school, the cold hard facts are usually given in a monotonous sequence which must be learnt by heart for an equally cold, and hard exam. If only in an exam, we were able to write down our experiences relating to the questions, instead of pouring out in great detail the scientific names for such uninvolved cells. On second thoughts, they do deserve a title for the work they do, and the efficiency with which they do it.

8

Having seen pints pints of blood – literay, worked with it done tests with it, studied it, mopped it up I find I am still fascinated by its story and yet I never have managed to get over that first 'squirm' when I see it. I've used the big words, learnt them, studied them but I think the simple down to earth language to describe this very important but common phenomena is far more interesting. My child learning a similar thing at school the other day amused us all by telling his brother, who had just grazed the skin off his knees, that there was a battle going on in the grazes. To imagine a battle – white soldiers v germs is so simple yet impresses me far more than what I know about the incident. I can never forget the importance of blood to the body – Lord knows it's been drilled in, in no uncertain terms, to such an extent that to lose a drop seems so extravagent. When I have seen trolley upon trolley of blood plasma at first I have felt sick but then I marvel at the importance of this, to somebody somewhere. When preparing drip bottles in a lab we inspect every litre for 'bits', dust particles – tiny flakes of glass and I have wondered at the importance of this, one tiny poticle allowed to get through would be introduced into a person blood stream via a vein. What an incredulous journey it would have floating along in that deep red sea where red corpuscles white soldiers continually guard the body. Such important practise an eliminating the bacteria, keeping the body warm, carrying oxygen & co_2 to all parts of the body, are going on continuously in everybody.

9

Blood, that vital part of our life, but how repulsive to see someone actually prick themselves, to deliberately cause themselves to bleed.

Part of me felt this lecture horrible. – Blood, the substance that made me feel sick at the thought and at the sight of deliberate bleeding.

Another part of me was inquisitive. It was exciting, interesting to know and see what goes on within our bodies. But even with my interest caught I felt somewhat repulsed – the war, the cannibalism of those cells make that red mass more than just a liquid. It is a civilisation on itself, with warriors, workers and invaders – each pursuing it's life and job. And yet we are told that this is silly, these cells have not a life that we know, can't work – but I rebel. In my imagination they can be as real as people – they *do* work and live.

10

I rush through this ever spilling endless ocean of life

It's not a nine to five job you know – you're on call all day long – dashing about, hardly get a chance to clean out my dissolving chambers last week, where we had such a rush on. It gets a bit boring though I mean once you've been around the body for your sort of introductory trip – you know the general ideas of what to do in the various situations it's just repetition. Mind you you don't get so many of the neutralising jobs now. But still I seem to get this kind of feeling of satisfaction when a few of us have glutenated the area and all of those rotten bacteria are stuck together in a bunch. You know I think we'd all be far better off if we stuck together more – make a kind of limphacytes union then we'd all have less hours to do and get the job done more efficiently. I remember one time when we had a big rush of bacteria – salminella I think it was and oh what a bother we had – the fibrinogen manufacturers were not a bit united so they could not produce enough fibrin, the phagocytes were all down the end and the anti-toxins were off sick – now if we had been united it would have been alright – white corpuscel being interviewed by red one.

11

Something which I usually associate with children coming crying to me with dripping finger or knee. With my fetching the cotton-wool and dettol – with 'oohs' and 'That hurts' and 'Don't do that Mummy'   Or with a nose bleed during the night and stained sheets and pillow-cases plunged into cold water ready to be washed tomorrow.

Not a thought of its use – its vital function in all our bodies except when we hear of someone dying of leukemia especially if it happens to be a person known to to, as I did. And then perhaps a passing thought like 'You'd think they could do something by now to prevent such things happening' and 'It's wicked to spend all that money on space-flights etc when it might have been used to save a life.'

I used to give blood at a Donor Centre until one day I dashed home quicker than I should have done and out again, and fainted in chapel. I know I thought about blood and lack of it quite often during the next few days, and found out a few things about it, really for the first time in my life.

Whilst I was listening to the talk I was thinking how unscientific and exciting the 'battle of the blood' sounded when put in a non-scientific way, and trying to think how it would have affected my reactions to the tale to have it put in cold scientific terms as I imagine scientists 'real' scientists would do. I'm fairly sure I would have struggled more to understand the processes involved in maintaining the body, but I don't think I would have enjoyed it so much.

Have just thought of that marvellous bit of a Tony Hancock T.V. show about Blood doning. Great.

Families

Compiled by Liz Cartland

The following pieces of work were done by a group of second-year pupils during a morning's work spent talking, writing, and reading about themselves and their parents and their families. There is a transcript of a tape-recording of some of their discussion, together with the pieces of writing completed by the end of the morning.

Let us look at them talking first.

1

Extract from a taped discussion about some of the children's own writing. Second-year pupils – four boys, two girls, no teacher present.

c: My grandfather, he's always watching telly, Cowboys and Indians.
d: Oh my . . .
r: Does he . . . ?
d: He's still going strong then?
c: Yeh.
r: Are you *sure* he doesn't do anything else?
c: Not really.
r: My grandfather used to play golf.
d: Mine never watched telly, never watched it at all.
a: I watch about $1\frac{1}{2}$ hours a night.
s: I watch that much.

A: Yes, I suppose it's quite a lot.

D: I watch Morecombe and Wise.

C: Yeh, that's a laugh.

D: Most programmes are useless.

R: Terrible.

C: My nanas are both going strong.

S: Mine died.

S: One of mine died in '63 or '64, I can't remember.

R: My dad's grandad, I can remember him, you know.

D: Your dad's *grandad*!

R: Yes, he was nice, I can remember quite a lot really.

A: Shall we read another one?

S: Yes, let's read Daniel's.

D: You read it.

R: I'll read it.

R. *reads*

My Grandfather

He stood deep in thought
　While the milk on the stove
Boiled over
　His eyes with no sentiment
Flickered
　Stared on and on and gone
An old chair creaked as he sank down
　And his mind ticked on.
In endless fields of thought
　Of great rivers so long
Of wrought iron bridges
　To cover the rolling mind
Of my grandfather.

S: That's good.

A: Very good.

S: Can I see it. I'll have to read it again.

C: Yer, let's see. [*Murmer of voices*]

　　[*Pause*]

S: It's very good. It's very true to life, true to his grandfather.

A: Do you know his grandfather then?

S: No, but all he's told me, he talks about him a lot.

G: I don't understand the last part, the bit, that line about 'wrought iron bridges'.

R: I think it's there because it sounds good. I read it and thought 'that's good' but then I thought 'well, what have wrought iron bridges to do with it?'

D: Well, I suppose, I suppose I did kind of, well, write it or it kind of came; but I think it is right.

S: Why?

D: Well, the main thing about him is he is like a bridge. I remember, well, he's always coped with things, climbed over obstacles, made kind of, well, bridges you see across, between things, between us, too. Do you see?

G: I suppose so.

S: I think I see. Grandparents are often easier to get on with than parents. They patch up quarrels, don't they?

D: Yes, it seems to be well, easier with them, they don't make such a big problem out of things.

A: My parents say my grandparents spoil me.

C: It's because they haven't got, well the responsibilities parents have got.

D: In some ways they're like children again.

A: Yes.

[*Laughter*]

D: 'Wrought iron' was because he does everything well and because in his days bridges were made not of, well were made of wrought iron not cement.

R: Yes. [*Confusion of voices*]

G: He's thinking of the past, isn't he, things like, that have gone before. He doesn't notice what's happening now. Old people are like that, my gran, she remembers everything when she was a girl, but not what happened yesterday.

S: Yes.

A: That's right.

R: Yes.

S: I wonder if it's true.

G: I think . . .

R: If what's true?

S: Well, sort of what they remember, like it was always better then, in their day, even the weather.

[*Laughter*]

A: Or else 'I didn't have all these things when I was a girl', and 'I wasn't allowed to do that', and 'Think yourself lucky'.

[*Laughter*]

R: Well, they can't just make it all up, though. It can't be, well, very nice to be old.

s: No, and not be able to do things any more.
d: We all change things that happen.
a: What do you mean?
d: Well, if I do something wrong, or get, well, you know, embarrassed, well I think about, and do it again and again in my mind. I sort of act it out.
g: Yes, I know.
   [*Murmur*]
d: I make it, well, better, till it stops worrying me.
   [*General murmur*]
g: His grandfather doesn't sound as if he's changing things, or making things up. He's just thinking and remembering. It's sad, it's a sad poem.
d: *I* don't think it's sad. You see, he does that. He's thinking and the milk boils over. He always has his eggs boiled hard. I don't think he's ever had a soft-boiled egg in his life.
s: Do you remember that poem about the grandfather *A Moment* . . .
r: Oh yes, *A Moment*
s: *A Moment of Respect*
d: That was good. *That* was a sad poem. It more describes . . .
r: Yes, I know, it describes better.
d: That bit, where they all move their watches on.
s: Yes they all, all the family depended on him.
d: Our family is like that.

Although comments based on this transcript alone could only be tentative, I think we can ask what differences there might be between work involved in this group discussing their own writing, and work where they would write just for the teacher or for an unspecified audience. We can also ask what are the constraints on the children. What are the implications of the absence of the teacher? This is not playground activity, but nor is it closely directed by, or mediated through the teacher.

At some time or another we all chat about our families, our memories of particular incidences involving them, about old people in general; we might even write about these things. The difference that this particular classroom context is making is that the often disparate activities of talk, reading and writing are brought closely together in a group sharing reasonably common purposes. They do not appear to be under pressure but they do feel that they have a job to do; early in the transcript, Anita recalls them to this. They have been left by the teacher to work together in this way; they are sufficiently interested in each other to do so and the teacher's absence means that she is not there to determine the results.

I think the transcript of their talk gives a sense of their willingness to share experiences and ideas; they are supportive of one another and a trust has been built up which enables, for example, Daniel to say:

Well, if I do something wrong, or get, well you know, embarrassed, well I I think about, and do it again and again in my mind. I sort of act it out . . . I make it well, better, till it stops worrying me.

The first comments on this tape are random, not really discussion, but Robert's reading of Daniel's poem 'My Grandfather' focuses their attention on the poem and on each other. They start listening to each other more attentively, they ask each other questions, wait for the answers, build on each other's points.

They seem to range in a relaxed and confident way between discussion of the poem, their own anecdotes, and also into the field of generalization:

He's thinking of the past, isn't he, things like that have gone before. He doesn't notice what's happening now. Old people are like that, my gran, she remembers everything when she was a girl, but not what happened yesterday.

In working in this group over a period of time, we had tried to establish a practice of discussing draft copies of pieces of writing, sharing some of the problems and possibilities of writing as an ongoing process. I think the emphasis in these discussions would have been in the area of 'come closer', 'what is it really like?', rather than 'how could we put this better?', but at times attention to perception about experience and attention to the processes of writing come very close together. As well as their 'sharing talk', this group looks closely at Daniel's poem: they push him to explain, they show interest in how the poem says as well as what it says and perhaps their explorations bring discovery for Daniel too about his own writing:

Well, I suppose, I suppose I did kind of, well, write it or it kind of came; but I think it is right. . . . Well, the main thing about him is he is like a bridge. I remember, well, he's always coped with things, climbed over obstacles, made kind of, well, bridges you see across, between things, between us too. Do you see?

Isn't this a big step? An imaginative leap involving both perception about his grandfather and about his own writing about him.

Talk about writing seems to have status in their conversation and they seem to think that the activity of writing is interesting and worthwhile in relation to their own experiences and ideas. In this kind of writing they do not appear to feel that their work is of a totally different order from that of the 'expert', the published writer. The poem they refer to in passing is Edwin Brock's 'A Moment of Respect'.

In turning now to some of the writing produced during this morning, I think it is interesting that although they have given each other support throughout their writing, working very closely together, each piece is nonetheless clearly their own, quite different and individual.

2 My Family

My sister, Anita, and I are always fighting. The arguement is usually her fault but I lose my temper very quickly. Our arguements are usually about little things for example the other day Anita said there were three buttons on our new television that were just for decoration. I said the makers would not put them there if they didn't have a use. We started fighting and she tried to fiddle with the buttons to prove it. We aren't supposed to touch the television so I tried to drag her away. She started screaming and we got into trouble. I usually get blamed because she cries and when I say she started it my father will tell me not to answer back or tell me I'm old enough to ignore her. That's easier said than done.

Sometimes she can be really spiteful. All I've got to do is say 'I like this record' when it's playing on the radio and she will immediately start singing across it. One day we had a fight and I found her throwing darts at all my Elvis Presley pin-ups. I yelled at her and my mother told me not to be so childish over a few pictures. I think a lot of parents expect to much of the eldest child.

When I was eight or nine I used to terrify Anita. When she had a head-ache I told her things like she had a rare disease and would die in a few years. I think all children do that kind of thing sometime. It gives you a feeling of power when you know you can make someone cry just by saying a few words.

I think if a husband and wife could swop over jobs for a day like they do in films there would be a lot less rows. In my opinion most fights between husband and wife are caused by one thinking he works twice as hard as the other and isn't appreciated.

At weekends I sometimes help my mother clean upstairs and I'm usually sitting down for a rest when my father comes back from golf. If the lounge isn't tidy he starts yelling at me to tidy up. He tells me I'm lazy and good-for-nothing and that I'll grow up helpless. If I say what about Anita who's usually playing he tells me it's got nothing to do with her and says 'you're so frightened that you're going to do something and Anita isn't'. If I'm feeling adventurous I say 'why don't you do something except play golf?' It was at about this stage that he used to hit me but he doesn't any more.

Sian *aged 12*

3 When I Was Three

When I was three I had a great passion for frogs. Whenever I saw one I would shut the dog in, because I was afraid that she would eat them. One day I saw a frog under our plum tree and being unable to pull the dog away ran for a jar to put the frog in. I ran all the way down to our house (a good 150 yards) collected an old fish bowl and ran back to the frog.

I managed to get it into the bowl but the dog kept dancing round me, so I started to run. About eight yards from the house I fell over and broke the bowl. The frog got away unharmed but I still have a mark on my right hand to prove that this happened.

I had just learned to walk up and down the stairs properly. Before I decended I would look behind me, to make sure that nobody would push me. Daddy called me to dinner I came from my bedroom to the top of the stairs, looked behind me and promptly fell, head over heels all the way down stairs.

I was more shocked than hurt but started crying. Daddy came out from carving and started laughing at me. 'I said he was horrid'

The Sea Serpent

I lie beneath the sea all day,
Writhing, squirming everyway.
I am the sailors bane and fear,
When storms are needed my head I rear.
And grunt and snarl,
And writh and sneer.
Then send the winds,
Both far and near.
And then I sink
To murky depths
And lie in wait
For the sinking wreks.

Deborah *aged 12*

4 Town Boy

The train flashed past green fields and country streams. Finaly it began to slow into the small country station of little Bramley.

But to Steve the prettyness of the country side meant nothing. The guard came up this is your stop sonny.

'Cor what a dump

'Well you best get down quick.

So Steve grabbed hold of his tatty suitcas and climbed down onto the station. The boy was about 11 years old with a pale freckled face dark curly hair and long skinny arms and legs.

He looked round and saw a tall sun tanned woman of about 40 approching him. 'Are you Steve

'Yeah you must be the old I mean me aunt Jane.'

'Thats right pick up your bag and follow me.

She strode out of the station where a pony and trap were waiting. Steve climbed up and they set off as they went through the village all village children stared.

Steve stuck his tongue out. Actually if the truth was know Steve was rather scared of staying here.

He was used to the dirt and smoke of the back streets of London. But he suffered from a chest complaint and could not cary on living there.

'You're to start the village school tomorrow Steve.

'School I aint going t no school. Next day he was taken to the school he sat at the back of the classroom doing nothing and then at break he went out side where all the other children started to push him around.

He punched one boy in the eye he were'nt scared he Steve Parker leder of the gas work gang were'nt scared of know country bumkins.

With that he ran to the open field of cows and opened the gate and ran through without closing the gate.

After a while he sat by a stream and Steve leader of the gas work gang cried. A sound behind him made him start up it was the boy he had hit his eye had swollen a great deal but he was smiling.

what do you want. I followed you so youde come back and be friends with us.

'Doya really mean that'.

Of coures we didn't mean to upset you well you never but I dont loike school never ave'

'Come on then whats youre name

'Steve whats you'ne?

'David

'Well Dave we better get back'

So the two boys went back. When Steve got home that night his aunt found a much happier less arrogant Steve. It must be the country air she sighed to herself as he tucked into a huge stew.

She looked at the small freckled face and saw the tear stain.

She nodded nowingly I think hell like it here.

Clive *aged 12*

5 A detestable Visit

I didn't wan't to go I knew it would be like this yak yak yak the hole time
Oh we'll only be half an hour said my mother. And we'd been at great
antie Ethels an hour and a half already and there were no sighns of mouving
so I sit there making dissapproving noises and wondering when dear auntie
is going to hand round those deliciose chocolate buiskets that sit enticingly
on the lace covered tablecloth. Its funny how the time used to go at great
aunt Ethels house to mum but it was the complete oposite for me. I used
to sigh fiddle with my fingers or even tap my feet in order to be noticed by
either one of them but neither of them ever did. I tried to but in to their
conversation to ask for another buiskuit but the occasian never arose, I
couldn't get a word in anywhere. I used to ask if we could go home when
auntie went out of the room to find a knitting pattern or some such thing,
but the answer was always in a minute or soon we'll go. As time wore on
my eyes wandered over the neat little room the little ornaments over the
fire place always caught my eye first I liked the golden elephant best but
I never got up to touch its smooth shiny body just in case auntie disaproved.
After that there was the little green bugeriegar tweeting away perched in
his cage like me I couldn't get away either only the diffrence was he was
happy. And then lastly there was the coockoo clock in the corner on the
wall and a little lady swung up and down on a swing underneath the clock.
She used to tick the seconds minutes hours away for me while I sat and
watched her jolly face go up and down. Then at last mum would get up and
say we had to be off I couldn't help showing the pleasure in my face by
giving a wide smile. But soon my pleasure distilled they were now talking
at the door for over ten minutes then just before we went auntie mums
auntie really used to rush in and make me a present of a bag of sweets
which always made me feel guilty and sorry for being pleased when we had
to go. But now everythings diffrent when we go to aunt Ethels. I quite
enjoy listening to their conversation and joining in and I no longer watch
the time pass by perhaps I'm growing up.

Karen *aged 12*

6 Granny

Jenny slammed the front door behind her after coming home from school.
'Friday again no more school for two whole days', she said. Jenny threw
her brief case across the hall kicked off her shoes and hung up her coat.
'Mum, I'm home', she called out. 'Come and have your tea dear', came a
voice from the kitchen. Jenny poked her head round the kitchen door.
'Bit early isnt it', she answered in a suprised voice. 'Yes dear, we're going
to pick up your gran, she's staying with us for a while' her mother explained

handing her a plate of susage and chips. 'The tables laid, eat your tea quickly your father will be in soon'. After she had eaten tea she quickly changed her clothes and they went to pick her grandmother up, by the time they had got home it was nearly eleven o'clock so Jenny went strait to bed. Jennys grandmother had never stayed with them before so it was a new experience for her. For the first day of her grans stay everything was fine, she was given money for sweets and she was peted and spoilt but the next day things began to change, first it was 'Jenny be a dear and go to the shops to get me some cough sweets' and then it was 'Jenny could you post this letter for me', and then there was 'Jen love could you go upstairs and get my glasses and book'. In the evening they were having tea and Jenny happened to mention that she didn't want to go to school, this was a fatal mistake, her gran gave her a lecture on how bad school was in her day and the distance she had to walk and how strict the teachers were. Jenny just sat saying yes and no in the right place at last the lecture was over and Jenny went off to do her home work. The next evening when Jenny came home from school she rushed through her homework so she could watch a certain programme, it was just comming on when her gran said 'turn over love I want to see the news'. Jenny was just about to argue when she stoped herself. Several times in the week her friend had come to play but they were driven away by her gran who un knowingly pestered their games by telling them they were playing it wrong or kept asking Jenny to do things. In the end Jenny could'nt stand it any longer, she asked her mother when her gran was going home. 'Don't worry dear she's going tomorrow answered her mother, thats why we never had her to live here, because of the uproar she would corse.

Gillian *aged 12*

Who is Peter?
Compiled by John Mole

Few things succeed like an apparition. A line stretches from the Cheshire Cat to Hamlet's ghost and beyond, into the beyond, and many teachers will be familiar with it. However, working with classes of the twelve to fourteen age group, I have found that the most popular apparition is oneself; children delight in discussing the possibilities of astral projection, metamorphosis and alter-ego, and like to consider the idea of haunting each other. So, we tell stories amongst ourselves and always, somewhere, I slip in an improvised spine-chiller, based on the doppel-ganger motif, about the man who meets himself, face to face in a deserted house and dies on the instant. At the same time, or maybe a little later, we might look at the fate of Wilde's Dorian Gray, read *Dr Jekyll and Mr Hyde* (perhaps getting each member of the class to write a character study of the former by the latter), Delmore Schwartz's poem 'The Heavy Bear who goes with Me', parts of Conrad's 'The Secret Sharer' and a poem of the same name by Thom Gunn; the list could go on, and nearly always we have taken Ralph, Jack and Piggy from *Lord of the Flies*, asking the question 'how complementary and/or necessary is each to the other?' as well as the passage in Richard Hughes's *A High Wind in Jamaica* where Emily explores the possibility of her being God.

The course this series of lessons takes is, as far as I am concerned, intuitively rather than consciously directed, but what I feel emerges is some kind of development from absorption in the supernatural to such personal considerations as – how many of me are there? What are the differences between us? What happens, or could happen, when we become incompatible? Put like that they may sound somewhat contrived but in the classroom context they usually seem real enough.

And so, to the main writing assignment (which I have introduced, on different occasions, both at the end and at the beginning of this set of lessons). The four pieces which follow it, all by thirteen-year-old children and obviously different in their approach, are, I think, as indicative as such a small set of illustrations can be of the variety I have come to expect from this particular subject. The first and second pieces are by eighth graders from a high school in New York. The third and fourth pieces are by second formers from a direct grant school.

'As he was looking across the street at the large house, a face appeared in one of the upper windows. Peter couldn't believe his eyes but the harder he stared the more it was true; that face was his own.'

An unusual occurrence, certainly, but what effect did it have on Peter? Was he frightened, amused, indifferent or what? There was nobody around for him to go to and talk with, and he was quite a long way from home. What did he think? What did he feel? What did he do? Using the above extract as your opening sentences, write a story which recounts Peter's experience in detail. Incidentally, who *is* Peter? It will be necessary to make him a real and human personality if your story is going to be successful. How do you make someone interesting when you are writing about him? Start by thinking yourself into his situation; – like Peter, you're on your own now.

1 It's only yourself
It's only yourself

'As he was looking across the street at the large house, a face appeared in one of the upper windows. Peter couldn't believe his eyes but the harder he stared the more it was true; that face was his own.'

Peter froze. He could feel a warm rushing of blood through his entire body.

A look of surprise and horror came to the face in the window. Peter managed to swallow a wad of saliva. The face in the window disappeared, leaving Peter looking at nothing.

Peter wanted to run home and hide his head in his mother's apron, but at the same time knew it was impossible. He was turning to go when a voice called him. A voice he had heard before. He turned to see a boy about his height, with the face he had seen in the window; his face. Peter was bewildered. On one hand, he had no reason to be afraid. The other boy obviously just *looked* like him. On the other hand, the boy looked too much like him. The two boys were now just two feet from each other. Peter forced himself to hold out his hand.

'I'm Peter Warton.'

There was an uneasy moment of silence before the other boy spoke.

'That's funny, m-m-my name's Peter, too.'

'Peter what?'

'Would you like to come inside?'

Peter W. wondered why Peter? hadn't answered his last question. However, he didn't want to seem unfriendly, so he stepped towards the house, pushing aside a thick outer fence which surrounded it.

'I guess we both realized how much alike we look,' said Peter?, a sligh note of laughter in his voice.

'Yea. This is a nice place you got here. Very nice.'

'Come up to my room.' The two boys went up a short flight of stairs to Peter ?'s room.

Peter W. sucked in a short breath of air in surprise. Peter ?'s bookcase was almost exactly like his.

'Uh, I, uh, I see you have many books. I recognize many of them.'

The two boys got better acquainted. They talked about subjects ranging from football to school. They got so involved with learning about each other, that they had forgotten the startling similarities between them.

Peter W. took a book out of the bookcase and turned to page 94. 'You know, when we first saw each other, an interesting theory I have read in this book came to my mind. It's all about parallel universes and stuff like that. Specifically, it says that time is divided into segments. All the segments are taking place at the exact same time, but one overlaps into the next. For instance, if I were swimming, and I drowned, I would automatically go into the next time segment. There I would go on swimming and living a normal life. Parents, brothers and sisters, aunts, uncles, etc. are all duplicated. However, in the old segment I would be very much dead.'

'That's all fine, but as far as I'm concerned, unless the theory is your own, it's no good.'

This was the first bad part Peter W. detected in Peter ?'s personality. Peter W. thought Peter ?'s last statement was most pompous. But aside from making a mental note, Peter W. paid it no more attention.

However, as the boys talked more and more, Peter W. disagreed more and more with Peter ?. Finally, to avoid an argument, Peter W. said, 'It's getting kinda late. I think I better go.'

'No, you're not going!'

'But Peter, I really must. I mean . . .'

Peter ? started walking slowly towards Peter W.

'Peter, I'm sorry I have to go, but . . . Peter, what are you doing? Peter, I . . .!'

Peter W. felt the same rushing of warm blood through his entire body as when he had first seen Peter ?.

When Peter W. next looked around he was alone.

Peter threw a book onto the floor of the library and ran out. The librarian, bewildered at the boy's action, went over to pick the book up.

'He's only 12 years old. Too young to be a student radical,' she laughed to herself. The librarian picked up the book and walked slowly to the section marked 'Biographies'. She looked for W. W for Warton. Peter Warton.

Chris *aged 13*

2

If Peter is the type that goes around seeing himself in windows of large houses across the street, he is:

(a) Eccentric – he has a taste for the bizarre.
(b) Conceited – he imagines these things to happen to himself rather than others, thus playing up his own importance in life.
(c) Lazy – there are certainly better things to do than go around staring at windows of large houses across the street either looking for, or seeing, yourself, and
(d) Intelligent – this sort of thing comes from reading too many Edgar Allan Poe stories in the fifth grade.

The reason that I have so been able to describe Peter is that I have been describing myself. This sort of thing has happened to me countless times, and generally for the same four reasons.

My eccentricity stems from the fact that, from early childhood, I was never able to fit into or agree with the norm. There being nothing else left to do, I competed with it.

My conceit emerged because in order to *successfully* compete with the norm, I certainly had to be a whole lot better.

My laziness stemmed from the conceit, in that if I were to be a whole lot better than the norm, I could not, in all pride, work as much as it.

The intelligence I considered to be a function of eccentricity, since most, if not all of the intelligent people I knew were real wierdos, so, if I were to be a good eccentric, I had to be intelligent.

The deucedly funny thing about all this is what it becomes with age. You would certainly think that after I understood all of this, I could correct it. But this is not true generally for two reasons. One, that this sort of personality has a way of growing on you, and, two, I figured that if I got rid of it, there would be nothing left: I would have to start from scratch, and that you see, would be contrary to all laziness.

This, in short, was Peter's predicament, unless, of course, the house across he street was dark, and Peter, being instead exceptionally stupid saw his reflection without suspecting it.

Victor *aged 13*

3

Peter was staying with his crusty old aunt Mabel in her small caretaker's house next to Burghley Towers. Burghley Towers was an old, rambling Elizabethan mansion owned by some remote aristocrat who insisted on keeping it for apparently no reason at all. Peter had only been in it once but knew it contained long, rambling, dusty corridors and was in a terrible state of repair.

One evening, just as the dusk was creeping up from the wood, Peter was contemplating the mansion from his bedroom window. As he was looking across at the large house, a face appeared in one of the upper windows. Peter couldn't believe his eyes but the harder he stared the more it was true; that face was his own.

For a moment or two he just stood there, aghast, watching the face. Somehow it lacked the healthy, robust colour of his own countenance. The face he saw framed against the musty darkness had more the colour of old parchments that might disintegrate at a touch. Suddenly the face disappeared.

Peter sank down onto his bed, he didn't know what to do. His eyes hadn't failed him, it really had been him. Him. It took him a long time to come to the decision to search Burghley Towers for the boy he had seen at the window. His aunt was out so he went downstairs into the kitchen and took the bunch of keys off the hook behind the door and then, as it was now virtually dark, he grabbed his torch before stepping out into the dark.

Just as he was fitting the huge key into the lock he paused. Did he really have to investigate? After all, his aunt would soon be back and perhaps it wasn't a face he had seen. But then he remembered the exact resemblence of the face to his own, curiosity overcame and he turned the key. The door swung silently open and he entered.

He was in a long, high hall and as the beam of his torch flicked from wall to wall he saw they were hung with tapestries. At one end was a gallery. He made his way across the hall and into a long narrow passageway. For a moment he stopped and listened to the silence. His torch was off now and he was in complete darkness. Not a sound. No, breathing. Was it his own? He stared into the darkness that seemed to completely cover his eyes like water. There was something near him, something right by him. Breathing. He switched on the torch. There was a scuffle and he thought he caught a glimpse of a foot disappearing round the corner. It was a full blooded chase now. The clang of running footsteps reverberated from the stone walls. A cold sweat broke out on Peter's brow. He was gaining. suddenly the footsteps stopped. This is it, thought Peter and leapt into the dead end with a loud 'Got you!' The torch beam flicked across the walls. There was no one there.

He shone his beam round behind him. 'Come out there!' he yelled. A complete silence. He retraced his steps to the last doorway. 'Must have got out here.' he muttered to assure himself although he knew full well that he had well passed this point before the footfalls stopped. . . .

He was in a large hall facing a great staircase which started in the centre of the room and splayed out when it reached the second floor. Peter sent his torch beam skipping about over the walls just to make sure that the mysterious intruder wasn't lurking in some shadowy corner. It had not yet occurred to Peter that the trespasser's exact resemblance of him was more than an incredible chance and not something so completely beyond him, so that the only feelings he had at present were morbid curiosity and a desire to punish the intruder. So he leapt up the stairs, two at a time. He reached the top and spotted a doorway that led to the gallery above the hall. He stood there, in the doorway as his torch beam searched the gallery, then, suddenly, he was there, caught in the beam of the torch. The boy Peter had seen from his bedroom window. He was dressed very oddly in a scarlet coat with a little sash round his waist and a very fancy lace cravat round his neck. He wore blue breeches down to just under his knees and from there on, silk stockings.

For a whole minute Peter stared at him. The boy squinted against the

light and held his arm over his eyes. Throughout the confrontation Peter
had an incredible feeling inside him – he felt that he was the boy caught in
the beam of light as well as himself. It was as if one battery was powering
two bulbs.

Then, suddenly, this was shattered by a sharp voice from below, in the
hall. 'Peter, what on earth are you doing up there?' It was Aunt Mabel.
For a fraction of a second he turned his head. When he looked round
again, the boy had disappeared.

William *aged 13*

4 The face

As he was looking across the street at the large house, a face appeared in
one of the upper windows. Peter couldn't believe his eyes but the harder
he stared, the more it was true; that face was his own. The features were his
own – mirrors didn't tell lies, he shaved each morning. But there was something about it that was very different; he knew the expression in those eyes
just wasn't quite like himself. The face wasn't smiling or laughing but a
strange mixture of the two with no feeling of mirth or jollity behind it but
a kind of stillness like a mask, putting the head into suspended animation.
The becalmed face did not stir or even fade . . .

. . . But Peter must have moved, because he found himself sitting upright
in a chair in his apartment. He knew he was distressed and he knew that the
face – his face – was causing him to be so. But he couldn't draw any con-
clusion other than that the face was in his mind and that his imagination
was for some reason telling him that his own personality, his real face's
expression, was wrong. The face was a mirror image of himself – in a
mirror made to distort. Somehow he felt that his own self was distorted and
that the mirror image was a photograph of the real Peter.

That night Peter dreamed of the face looking out from the remote
window of the great house. He saw it as if photos were being shown to
him of smiles that would have turned into laughs had only they been seen
a little later. The face, his own face, was happy in a morose sort of way.
And all through the dream Peter subconsciously knew he was being privil-
eged to see himself.

It was in the evening of the next day when Peter remembered the face
and his dream and in a flash he realised what it all was. The large house
represented his mind and the small window was its uttermost recess. This
small part of his mind had conquered the rest of it because it was the only
unpoisoned part. He had been poisoned by bitterness at the death of his
parents and had not lost his harsh words used at the orphanage ten years
gone till now he realised how friendless he was. The face was the first nine

years of his life when he was used to enjoying himself. The dead happiness on the face was prevented from becoming real by his stupidity and unwillingness to forget his parents in the same way as the orphans he lived with. Now Peter was as most people are. A face in an upper window had changed his whole life.

John *aged 13*

Poetry and the sixth form

Compiled by John Mole

The following transcript is made from part of a taped discussion, the speakers being members of my sixth-form 'Writers Workshop' which meets regularly on an informal club basis. In the knowledge that there is little opportunity for older children to develop their interest in imaginative writing during school hours, the course has been offered as part of the General Studies programme – at a direct grant school – and is aimed at encouraging those still seriously engaged upon this activity. A large amount of time is spent circulating, reading and criticizing members' work and not too much on more general theory unless it arises from the demands made by a particular piece of writing under consideration. The emphasis is technical and empirical; each member is trying to become better acquainted with the method and discipline implicit in his own private effort, hence the somewhat awkward progress of this discussion in which – at various points – continuity may seem to give way to obsession. To add variety – as well as to offer the group the opportunity of meeting, learning from and perhaps even identifying with professionals – practising writers have been invited to take over a session and guide it in whatever direction they wish; some have read their own work, answering questions on it and accepting tentative body-blows, while others have chosen to comment on work offered for their opinion. In the discussion, Tony's reference to the American poet Louis Simpson – one of our guests – gives a passing indication of how much can be gained by a young practitioner from meeting with a sympathetic 'graduate'; it is stimulating to disagree with a good writer who also happens to be patient – it helps one towards the shaping of independent views.

The poem 'Tube Train Trauma', which led us into this discussion, can be found earlier (in the section 'Sharing Experience') and, to give a further dimension to some of the voices heard, I have appended poems by four of the most prominent.

1

SELF: Would you like to talk a bit about this distinction you made earlier between 'public' and 'private'?

TONY: Well, I think it's really emotions. I don't think I can write a poem about an ex-girlfriend in a public fashion. I don't think I could write what I call a 'private' poem about a journey in a train, you know, in which I have all these erotic and sensuous fantasies . . .

[*Laughter*]

SELF: . . . and which you want to share with the world you suspect has those fantasies too . . .

TONY: Yes, I think what I call 'private' poems are more personal emotions. I mean it's possible that people could probably identify with them – have the same emotions – but I don't think they're as readily identifiable with as, say, 'Tube Train'.

SIMON: I don't agree.

DANNY: I don't agree at all.

SIMON: For instance, the pleasure one can get from pin-pointing one's own emotions and reactions to events can be shared with other people – that you can get pleasure from showing it to other people and they can gain pleasure from recognizing it. . . .

TONY: Yes, I know what you mean – I'm not saying that just because I write something mainly for myself I don't want to share it. I think 'Tube Train' is what I would more readily issue . . . for public consumption, if you like.

DANNY: It's not only that. I don't think there are public and private poems – it's just *one* – but any poem which has to have a private theme I want positively to scream to everyone else because when I do write a poem with that sort of sentiment . . . I want to communicate it . . . .

NIGEL: . . . You've got to get it down, and afterwards you can identify with what you felt at that time and maybe you can show them round to someone else and it doesn't matter what they say about them – you don't care because they're very special emotions brought back by reading it. That's what I always find – no matter what anybody else says about these sort of things – you know they're just irrelevant because they mean something very special to you.

SELF: Like 'That's *our* tune' . . .

NIGEL: Yes, that sort of thing. Yes.

SIMON: It's a basic safety mechanism of people not being able to challenge your reaction . . .

[*General laughter*]

you've got yourself to fall back on. You know, 'that's *me*.'

NIGEL: Oh yes.

PAUL: It depends on your own attitudes, though, doesn't it. I mean if it's really a truly personal poem you can write what you like, you can write gibberish . . . if you're not going to show it to anyone, OK write down gibberish.

ANDY: What's the function of writing a private poem, though?

DANNY: Exorcizing ghosts.

PAUL: It's a catharsis.

ANDY: I don't see why it should have any form or why it should be grammatically correct or . . . judge it on whether it sounds pretentious or not. I mean, if it's real, if it's personal and it's purely cathartic then really it can't be pretentious.

SIMON: I think it becomes an innate sort of process – that you write partly for other people, that externalization of your feelings means that you're placing them at someone else's disposal.

DANNY: It's terrible, actually. After a while you find you're bringing out all your innermost emotions and sticking them on bits of card for people to throw darts at – you know, it's really a sort of masochistic process in the end.

PAUL: But doesn't the fact that you're writing down your innermost emotions – I find – sort of lessen their virulence to some extent. I mean if I'm. . . .

DANNY: No, not really lessen it. It helps you to understand them a bit.

PAUL: Look, I'm being – say – very jealous of somebody and I write down a poem saying the jealousy, then the jealousy diminishes. I find that happens. I don't care if people throw darts.

ANDY: I find it pretentious just to write something very private down on paper. I think that by putting it down on paper you're *shaping* it, an emotion, by just forming words really, and it becomes pretentious.

PAUL: Why? Why?

ANDY: Yes, well, perhaps this is because I can't express myself very well on paper anyway but I find that whenever I write, *try* and write, an emotion down as exactly as possible – as soon as it gets down on paper it's in some way changed.

PAUL: That's the challenge isn't it? Once you've crystallized an emotion, as Danny said earlier, you exorcize it.

ANDY: But crystallization of emotion is false in itself. Emotions aren't crystallized.

PAUL: But if you write anything subjective while you're in the grip of a very strong emotion that emotion comes through in the poem, even if it's in a changed form.

ANDY: It might come through but it depends on other people being able to identify by you giving them a few *clues*. Really, people aren't communicating in poetry at all, they're working out their hang-ups in a minor way by reassuring themselves that their emotions are normal by putting them down on paper. It's much more reassuring.

PAUL: No, isn't it that they are putting them down to make sure that their emotions are emotions?

SIMON: I don't think that's a motivation. I think that's a rationalization.

SELF: Is all poetry about 'emotions' and 'hang-ups'? Is it basically a matter of writing about *thwarted* love, and *thwarted* this and that? Always about something that is wrong and never about something that's right?

SIMON: Personally, I think that I write more poems when I've got things to be worried about than when I haven't.

DANNY: Poetry's a very good way of getting out of a depression, or trying to get out of a depression.

SELF: Do you find it 'cheers you up'?

SIMON: It cheers me up if I'm proud of what I've written.

ANDY: I.e. it diverts him from what's bothering him.

DANNY: But it's quite an achievement to make something positive out of something which is very negative. Unfortunately, though, I find that all the poems I write when I'm hung-up aren't very good. Or at least they need a lot of chopping and changing afterwards.

PAUL: You've got to write poems when you've got over the worst of it but before the memory goes.

SELF: Are there any particular circumstances you find yourselves writing under? Particular places? Times of day? What sort of conditions do you impose upon yourselves while writing?

TONY: Personally, I don't impose conditions. Louis Simpson said that no poet should really wait for inspiration because you end up never writing anything. I don't agree with that so much.

PAUL: I don't think it's so much waiting for inspiration as waiting for an urge to write. I mean, I get urges to write at peculiar times and in peculiar places. The urge to write is there. You write what comes into your head.

SIMON: I largely write not having planned what I'm going to say but there are occasions when I feel I must write about some situation, some feelings, largely because I feel I must indulge in those feelings.

SELF: How does writing enable you to indulge more than simply lying on your back and mulling it over in your mind?

SIMON: I don't know. I just find – writing poems – you can really indulge in them. They're a mirror.

EDDIE: Surely a lot of what you write – you don't know what you've written until you've written it, and then you look at it and you find out what your emotions really are. It clarifies the whole situation.

TONY: I don't look on writing poetry as an effort.

DANNY: I write when I want to write. If I want to write I find it easy. If for some reason I should sit down and say 'right, I'm going to write a poem' and I can't get the words out, then I don't write it. There's nothing *to* write. If there *is* something to write, then it'll come.

SELF: Suppose you find that the most important thing ever is there underneath and it won't come – you get patient, do you, and you say 'well, it'll come some other time'?

DANNY: Yes.

2 Harvest Moon

Fat and creamy in the shrouding clouds,
Moon wobbles into the sky
Sprinkling black with yellowness.
There are wild pigs in the garden tonight
And frogs, and we must not wander from the path
For fear of sudden attack.
The warlocks and werewolves all conspire
Around inverted crosses, while witches
And bats flit across the empty fields.
We huddle by the fire, breath stinking
Of garlic, clutching hands. . . . waiting
For the dark to crack, in silence.

At length,
As the water unfreezes
And the fish awake,
As the air unthickens
And the stiff birds break cover,
As the flowers cautiously decide to open,
And as the fragile statuary of night splits
And dawn flows by,
We loosen grips, then smile, then cry.

Danny Friedman

3 Tangiers '69-'70

Kasbah, cous-cous and kif . . .
City of reds and browns.
Paralysis,

Of jarrowmen on street-corners,
And bruised fly-specked fruit,
Of living fowl surrounded by deadfellows,
And orchids amongst the grey stone.
Glory and mystery of old,
Now tarnished, like the market's wares.
Breeding-ground of childbeggars
Moaning for handouts, in the dust,
On streets irrigated by filth-streams.
And the cats, purring, satisfied, on hotel lawns,
Yawning, preening themselves in the grime,
Scorn their surroundings: the rulers of Tangiers.

Tony Bard

4 The Firewalkers

beneath charred cinders
coalblack valleys of night
the firewalkers raise their
gravel heads
and quirk an eyebrow at the scornful moon
wallowing in their pact
content to be a part of
salamander genesis
phoenix birth
asking for the rocks
of living clay
with which to mould the goal
that tinkles in the dark
teasing just beyond the reach

Paul Leigh

5 Night in Cambridge

My hands clasped round a bowl of chocolate
I sniff the window-boxed night.

A brawny shadow
Gurgles yellow into his proud scarf
Globs of belched boredom
Dregs of a jolly evening
Where men are men
And women's place is on the touchline.

Now
Stony slabs
Stamp icily on his feet
Leaving imprints of dog-shit and belated oaths.
His stomach retches
Under the punch of the wind
And he bends, frosty-eyed,
Over his mess.
Under the steely shafts of lamplight
He shivers another gutful against the post
Then stands still – like a frozen scarecrow.

Slowly, I turn back towards the fire,
My hands clasped round my bowl of chocolate.

Andy Forrester

References and Further Reading

BARTHES, R. (1967), *Writing Degree Zero*, trans. A. Lavers and C. Smith, Cape.

BARNES, D., BRITTON, J., ROSEN, H., and the LATE (1971), *Language, the Learner and the School*, Penguin, rev. edn.

BERNSTEIN, B. (1971), *Class, Codes and Control*, Routledge & Kegan Paul.

BRITTON, J. (ed.) (1967), *Talking and Writing*, Methuen.

BRITTON, J. (1970), *Language and Learning*, Allen Lane The Penguin Press; Penguin, 1972.

BRITTON, J. (1971), 'What's the use?', in A. M. Wilkinson (ed.), 'The context of language', *Educational Review*, vol. 23, no. 3.

BROWN, R., and BELLUGI, U. (1964), 'Three processes in the child's requisition of syntax', *Harvard Educational Review*, vol. 34, no. 2.

BURGESS, T. (1971a), 'Story and teller', *London Institute of Education Bulletin*, no. 24.

BURGESS, T. (1971b), 'Kinds of writing', *English in Education*, vol. 5, no. 2.

CLEGG, A. B. (ed.) (1964), *The Excitement of Writing*, Chatto & Windus.

COSIN, B. R., DALE, I. R., ESLAND, G. M., and SWIFT, D. F. (eds.) (1971), *School and Society*, Routledge & Kegan Paul in association with the Open University Press.

CREBER, J. W. P. (1972), *Lost for Words*, Penguin.

DRUCE, R. (1965), *The Eye of Innocence*, Brockhampton Press.

EHRENZWEIG, A. (1967), *The Hidden Order of Art*, Weidenfeld & Nicolson.

EMIG, J. (1971), *Composing Processes of Twelfth Graders*, NCTE.

FISHMAN, J. (ed.) (1968), *Readings in the Sociology of Language*, Mouton.

FORD, B. (ed.) (1963), *Young Writers, Young Readers*, Hutchinson, rev. edn.

GIGLIOLI, P. P. (ed.) (1972), *Language and Social Context*, Penguin.

GOFFMAN, E. (1964), 'The neglected situation', *American Anthropologist*, vol. 66, no. 6. Reprinted in B. R. Cosin, I. R. Dale, G. M. Esland, D. E. Swift (eds.) (1971), *School and Society*, Routledge & Kegan Paul.

GOFFMAN, E. (1969), *The Presentation of Self in Everyday Life*, Allen Lane The Penguin Press; Penguin, 1972.

GUMPERZ, J. (1968), 'The speech community', in *International Encyclopedia of the Social Sciences*, Macmillan.

GUMPERZ, J., and HYMES, D. (eds.) (1971), *Directions in Sociolinguistics*, Holt, Rinehart & Winston.

HALLIDAY, M. A. K. (1971), 'Language in a social perspective', in A. M. Wilkinson (ed.), 'The context of language', *Educational Review*, vol. 23, no. 3.

HANNAM, C., SMYTH, P., and STEPHENSON, N. (1971), *Young Teachers and Reluctant Learners*, Penguin.

HARDING, D. W. (1937), 'The role of the onlooker', *Scrutiny*, vol. 6, no. 3.

HARDING, D. W. (1963), *Experience into Words*, Chatto & Windus.

HOLBROOK, D. (1961), *English for Maturity*, Cambridge University Press.

HOLBROOK, D. (1964), *English for the Rejected*, Cambridge University Press.

HYMES, D. (ed.) (1964), *Language in Culture and Society*, Harper & Row.

JONES, A., and MULFORD, J. (eds.) (1972), *Children Using Language*, Oxford University Press.

JOOS M. (1961), *The Five Clocks*, Monton.

KELLY, G. A. (1963), *A Theory of Personality*, Norton.

KOHL, H. (1968), *36 Children*, Gollancz; Penguin, 1971.

KUHN, T. S. (1970), *The Structure of Scientific Revolutions*, University of Chicago Press, rev. edn.

LABOV, W. (1969), 'The logic of nonstandard English', *Georgetown Monographs on Language and Linguistics*, vol. 22. Also abridged in P. P. Giglioli (ed.), *Language and Social Context*, Penguin, 1972.

LANGER, S. K. (1960), *Philosophy in a New Key*, Harvard University Press, 3rd edn.

LANGER, S. K. (1967), *Mind, An Essay on Human Feeling*, vol. 1, Johns Hopkins Press.

LAWTON, D. (1968), *Social Class, Language and Education*, Routledge & Kegan Paul.

LENNEBURG, E. N. (ed.) (1964), *New Directions in the Study of Language*, MIT Press.

McLEOD, A. (1969), 'This is what came out', *English in Education*, vol. 3, no. 3.

MARTIN, N. (1971a), 'The process of writing', *ATE Journal*, Easter.

MARTIN, N. (1971b), 'What are they up to?', in A. Jones and J. Mulford (eds.), *Children Using Language*, Oxford University Press.

MARTIN, N. (1972), 'Children and stories: their own and other people's', *English in Education*, vol. 6, no. 2.

MOFFETT, J. (1968), *Teaching: The Universe of Discourse*, Houghton Mifflin.

OAKESHOTT, M. (1959), *The Voice of Poetry in the Conversation of Mankind*, Bowes & Bowes. Reprinted in M. Oakeshott, *Rationalism in Politics*, Methuen, 1962.

PIAGET, J. (1951), *Play, Dreams and Imitation in Childhood*, trans. C. Gattegno and F. M. Hodgson, Heinemann.

PIAGET, J. (1959), *Language and Thought of the Child*, trans. M. Gabain, Routledge & Kegan Paul.

POLANYI, M. (1958), *Personal Knowledge: Towards a Post-Critical Philosophy*,

PRIDE, J., and HOLMES, J. (eds.) (1972), *Sociolinguistics*, Penguin.

Routledge & Kegan Paul.

ROSEN, H. (1971), 'Messages and message-makers', in *English in Education*, vol. 5, no. 2.

SAPIR, E. (1961), *Culture, Language and Personality*, University of California Press.

STUART, S. (1969), *Say*, Nelson.

VYGOTSKY, L. S. (1962), *Thought and Language*, trans. Hanfmann and Vakar, MIT Press.

YOUNG, M. F. D. (ed.) (1971), *Knowledge and Control*, Collier Macmillan.

The Language of Primary School Children

Connie and Harold Rosen

What is the role of the teacher in fostering language development? Are working-class children really linguistically deprived? What is the relationship between the language of the school and that of the community? Does the 'progressive' primary school hold children back? What are stories for? Do drama and language mix?

This book is based on a large collection of material gathered over two years as part of the Schools Council Project on Language Development in the Primary School. It gives priority to the discussion of actual material produced in primary schools, and its main aim is to select for attention the most promising ways in which language is seen playing a vital part in learning. But it is also concerned to place this material within a framework of controversial themes and theoretical issues.

Few 'official reports' are as lively, as humane and as readable as this one. Its discussion of children in actual learning situations is both sensitive and practical; its account of the theoretical issues both wide-ranging and clear.

Language and Learning

James Britton

From the moment the child first speaks – first attaches a sound to an object or a person – language plays a significant and central part in his development. His speech is, of course, a means of communication; and yet the stress in this book is on the importance of speech, not to his listeners, but to himself. It shows, for example, that much of his behaviour consists in doing what he has told himself to do; that the world he sees and acts in is a world largely called into existence by words of his own speaking; that it is by speech, from infancy, that man turns a habitat into an environment.

Language and Learning is the outcome of James Britton's attempts to understand in the light of many theories, observations and experiments, and of his own first-hand experience as parent and teacher, the observable behaviour of children as they grow up.

'Parent and teacher alike will find the most directly appealing material, as the theoretical complexities of language acquisition and use are patiently presented and most skilfully and entertainingly illustrated with examples from children's speech and writing' *Educational Review*